Shattered Pieces
From
Broken2Blessed

Helena Lewis-Norman

Scripture quotations marked (AMP) are taken from the Amplified Bible, Copyright © 1954, 1958, 1962, 1964, 1965, 1987 by The Lockman Foundation. Used by permission.

Scripture quotations marked with ESV are from The ESV® Bible (The Holy Bible, English Standard Version®), copyright © 2001 by Crossway, a publishing ministry of Good News Publishers. Used by permission. All rights reserved.

Scripture quotations marked (NIV) are taken from the Holy Bible, New International Version®, NIV®. Copyright © 1973, 1978, 1984, 2011 by Biblica, Inc.™ Used by permission of Zondervan. All rights reserved worldwide. www.zondervan.com The "NIV" and "New International Version" are trademarks registered in the United States Patent and Trademark Office by Biblica, Inc.™

Scripture quotations marked (NLT) are taken from the Holy Bible, New Living Translation, copyright ©1996, 2004, 2015 by Tyndale House Foundation. Used by permission of Tyndale House Publishers, Inc., Carol Stream, Illinois 60188. All rights reserved.

Scripture taken from the New King James Version®. Copyright © 1982 by Thomas Nelson. Used by permission. All rights reserved.

Copyright © 2019 Helena Lewis-Norman

All rights reserved.

ISBN-13: 978-1-7325363-6-4

In honor and loving memory of
Joyce Lewis – My sweet Mother
Sha'Toriya Lewis-Foley – My beloved Angel and Daughter
Mr. Esau Lewis – My Grandfather
Trinia James – My Pastor and Spiritual Mother

Contents

Acknowledgements i

Foreword ii

Chapter 1 The Initial "Broken Piece" 1

Chapter 2 The "Cause of the Break" 4

Chapter 3 The Puzzle—How Do All the Pieces Fit? 7

Chapter 4 Picking up the Pieces 14

Chapter 5 Living in the Moment 16

Chapter 6 The Clean Up 24

Chapter 7 Shattered Identity 30

Chapter 8 Forgiveness is the Key 44

Chapter 9 Financial Break (Hardship) 50

Chapter 10 The Mental Break 55

Chapter 11 The Enemy of the Mind 66

Chapter 12 Suffering in Silence 90

Chapter 13 Failure is not Fatal 117

Chapter 14 Faith through the Fire 142

About the Author 172

Acknowledgements

I'm eternally grateful to my entire family, who supported me during this time to complete the work of my book. My super supportive husband, Mr. Gerald Norman, my beautiful daughters, MaKayla and Jaslin. My father Mr. Henry Lewis, his unconditional love has helped me succeed in life. My wonderful siblings John and Anthony Lewis, my sister and rock LaJoyce Timmons. And all of my extended family.

A Special Thank You to my Refiner's Fire Church Family. Your Love and Support has been instrumental on this journey. I love each of you.

Dr. Tonya Cunningham, I'm forever indebted to you. Thank you for being the navigating piece to connect me to my process to wholeness.

And thank you Lisa Bell of Radical Women for the hard work of editing and pulling this book together for publishing. With your expertise, this book is now available for God to use with many who need to put back together the shattered pieces of their lives.

Foreword

Life happens to all of us. At some point in time, something will happen to shatter your dreams, your faith, and yes your whole life. Tragedy, hurt, and brokenness crosses all socioeconomic boundaries, leaving us feeling hopeless. So it doesn't matter who you are. Somewhere along your journey, life will deal you a hand that you don't know how to play. It is at this moment that your entire life hinges upon your decision. Will you react and continue to do the same things you've always done such as avoid painful times in your life? Or, will you respond by doing something different and deal with the broken pieces in your life?

Shattered Pieces: from Broken 2 Blessed is a book that contains powerful practical and spiritual insights on how to take the broken pieces of your life and put them back together again in a healthy manner. As you read this book, you will take a journey with the author and explore the different types of life breaks that have shattered your world into pieces, causing you to view life through different lenses. Reading this book will empower you to identify the broken places and spaces in your life and then respond by getting the proper help that's needed to heal.

I have known Helena for many years as a colleague in ministry and now a friend. I affectionately know her as "Shawn." I remember the day she shared with me that her 24-year-old daughter, Tori, died. I immediately began to pray for her and hoped that she would get grief counseling to help her on her grief journey. As most people do, Helena fell into the trap that our culture and society set for us, which is to avoid dealing with loss, pain, and suffering. As spiritual leaders, the expectation is that we should pray about it and then pretend as if nothing life shattering happened to us. But how do you move on when your life has changed drastically in a moment? This question sent Helena on a downward spiral, searching for answers on how to live this life without her beloved daughter. Helena is a strong prayer warrior and intercessor but quickly realized prayer alone did not help her transition from loss to her blessed life. The moment she was ready to face her grief and pain and confront her multiple losses was the moment her healing journey began. For one year, I met with Helena weekly for grief counseling. She submitted to the process, did her grief work, and thus she is living a healthy, vibrant, and blessed life after brokenness. Her pain has now become her passion, and she is helping others through their broken places in life.

This book is a must read, especially for all in leadership because leaders have a tendency to neglect self-care to care for others. It offers a blueprint for healing to those in the Body of Christ and beyond. As we are instructed to do when flying in an airplane, in case of an emergency, put the oxygen mask on yourself first before putting it on your neighbor.

Enjoy your healing journey with new author, Helena Norman.

Dr. Tonya Cunningham
The Grief Doctor
Tonya Cunningham Ministries

There IS life after loss, it's just a different one!

Chapter 1
The Initial "Broken Piece"

When life deals you a hand you can't play, even the jokers have no value. What you are experiencing feels like the joke is on you.

In this moment of time, we define life as being so unfair. How do I recover from this unbearable heartache called the **"break?"** The break that shattered my dreams and visions of what I thought life was supposed to be. As you read this book, I want us to take a journey together—a journey exploring the different types of **Life Breaks** that **shattered** your world into pieces, causing you to view life, people, circumstances, your faith in God and most of all, how you viewed yourself differently before the break. The truth is, when we have one break in our lives, it opens the door to emotions we left suppressed from previous hurts and disappointments, not realizing the damage done.

In life, we all have experienced different types of unexpected **"breaks"** such as divorce, unemployment, the loss of a parent, spouse or child, relationship, a bad breakup, broken engagement, sickness, financial distress, and even the loss of a church or pastor. Often people say, "Get over it and move on." As if you don't desperately want to do exactly that.

Ironically, the people using those words haven't experienced pain from the piece of life you are experiencing at that very moment. Get over it, and move on—easier said than done, right?

Understand a crucial truth—all the different types of breaks that left your life **shattered** caused guilt, depression, suicidal thoughts, loneliness and betrayal. Ask yourself, "How did I get here?"

Glad you asked.

Your life break wasn't caused by you doing something terrible. Sometimes that's exactly it—LIFE happened. Realize death is part of life. Yes, that was hard for me to say, but it's true. Not just death from illness or a sudden event, but there's also the end of a marriage or long-time relationship you invested in. When it comes to an end, it feels like a death. You have to mourn and grieve through the process, accepting the fact it's over, and your life drastically changed—with or without your permission.

Life's unexpected turns can cause things to become utterly chaotic and dramatic.

While enduring these moments of uncertainty, you can sometimes forget about how to take care of yourself physically and mentally. Stress sets in, and before you know it, you are suffering from certain health challenges, high blood pressure, diabetes, heart problems, mental illness, etc. They all can stem from a single traumatic change of life you can't undo.

In addition, breaks don't always come as single events. Often they arrive in pairs, or one precipitates another until you have an avalanche of breaks, snowballing down on you, which is why the physical impact may be worse than if you have only one trauma happening.

For the sake of argument, we can look at one break without accompanying events. And in all honesty, one break can be enough to send even the strongest person tumbling over the edge. With that in mind, let's take the first step of our journey—the first step in picking up the pieces of our shattered hearts.

Chapter 2
The "Cause of the Break"

Was life cracked before the break or shattering?

Sometimes we can have cracks in certain areas of our lives before the break.

What do you mean?

I'm glad you asked.

Let's use an example of broken trust. As a little girl, I was teased and called Buckee Beaver because of my overbite. Funny now with a massive travel stop called Buc-ee's. It's one of my favorite places to stop when traveling to East Texas. If you've never been to one, you have to stop for a visit. This place has food, goodies, gifts and gasoline—everything in one place, plus so many clean restroom stalls, you never have to wait. Now that little beaver and his teeth earn a whole lot of money. So who's joking now?

From around the age of 10, up until my senior year of high school, other kids mercilessly teased me. Now forty years later, there's a popular place with the name that caused me so much pain and to lose my self-esteem. What a crazy thought.

I begged my parents to take me to the dentist to get braces. At the time, it was expensive, but they didn't have a clue about the torment I went through. Finally, after graduation, as I experienced this horrible toothache, my parents took me to the dentist.

I didn't hesitate to ask the dentist a burning question. "Can you fix my teeth?"

The rest is history. But the damage was already done. The crack was already there in my emotions, in the foundation of who I was. Although my overbite was gone, the pain remained. However, I tucked it inside a hidden place called "broken trust," which affected other areas of my life. From that point, I was never going to be teased again. Now I'm in control.

My transformation began on the outside, but the inside was still broken from the words of cruelty. Someone once told me, "Words are like feathers. Once they are released, you can never get them back."

I believe one of the greatest betrayals is the broken trust of a friend or loved one. Trust is defined as confidence (faith) placed in someone or something in which you can rely on, believe in and be assured they will do you no harm. Betrayal is one of the most common **"trust breakers"** that leaves an aftermath of devastation in the lives of so many people. It comes in many types and levels.

The root and cause of betrayal always lead back to the **"CRACK."** This hurt is like no other. It leaves a wound and hole in your life, "**shattering your heart**," which is the common denominator to unforgiveness—a mad disease all by itself. Why did I call it a disease? Because unforgiveness sets up infections in your heart. This is where we make others pay for the damage someone else did.

And next, we have to figure out what to do with all those pieces of our shattered heart.

Chapter 3
The Puzzle—How Do All the Pieces Fit?

    Like a puzzle you dump out of a box, the more pieces to the puzzle, the longer it takes to put it together. Each piece was strategically designed to create something beautiful. However, it's hard to see the final result when pieces lay spread out all over the place.

    My mother would sit for hours at the kitchen table as she worked on different puzzles. I don't know when this became a favorite hobby for her. I believe it started when someone gave her a puzzle for a Christmas gift. She soon discovered she enjoyed putting puzzles together in her quiet time.

    This hobby of hers became some of the most memorable times I spent with my mother, having long talks while trying to find the right piece to the round corners of the puzzle. I never had that much patience. However, during these times, I discovered putting the puzzle together wasn't all that bad. Actually, it felt pretty rewarding when I found a piece that fit.

    Mother always sat the puzzle box on top of the cake

plate on the kitchen table. After she dumped the majority of pieces out, she wanted a view of the picture, which was displayed on the front of the puzzle box. She glanced up at the box, then looked down at the pieces. After a minute, she glanced up again, and then her voice broke the silence. "That's the final outcome."

I complained about how hard it was to figure out what goes where.

She responded, "First look at the color, then the shape"

Of course, I tried her concept with absolutely NO PATIENCE.

"It's all in the colors," she gently encouraged.

I especially didn't like the multicolored pieces—they were too difficult. The smaller the pieces, the more difficult the puzzle came together.

I told mother, "It's easier when the pieces are larger."

She just laughed.

I remember the different types of scenery from the puzzles. One was a stunning garden. Then there was an exquisite flower pot. And one of my personal favorites—the green pasture with magnificent trees surrounded by blue water.

Each time, Mother found a puzzle more difficult than the one she completed before. It became challenging for her, and I never figured out why she wanted to get a 1200-piece puzzle when it took her months to put the 1000-piece scene together.

Over the years during those times at the table, Mother listened to my heart. Many others who came to visit received an invitation to sit at the table. While talking, they found themselves picking up a piece of the puzzle, trying to figure out where that piece fit. At times, many pieces of the puzzle remained in the box. We dug through the box to see if we could find the next piece that fit.

One day after Mother got one of her first largest puzzles completed, we tried to move it from the kitchen table to the back room. The puzzle began to fall apart. The cake plate holding the box fell, hit the floor and shattered while she tried to save the puzzle. She was more concerned about the puzzle than the cake plate because she spent countless hours working on the puzzle, trying to create the vision of the picture she saw on the outside of the box.

Can you agree that's how life can be sometimes, like a puzzle? Right at the time you think you got all the pieces snapped in the right place, you make one move. And what held things together hit the floor and shattered, causing you to face challenges you didn't think you would ever encounter.

As I worked on writing this particular chapter, I was encouraged and greatly overwhelmed as I read a post on social media by Mr. Dominique Hunter (one of my many sons). He shared his puzzle experience. I asked for permission to share his words with the readers of my book. He was excited and gracious to share this great revelation:

One day I was at work putting together a puzzle just to kill time (grown kid). I've never been that great at big puzzles, but the competitive nature in me pushed me to go for it anyway. As predicted within myself, I was struggling with where certain pieces belonged even having the finished product on the cover of the box

Like any normal person, I started finding pieces that match. Things started picking up, and the puzzle was coming together. However, there were still some misplaced pieces that slowed me down. After evaluating the color scheme, background, and surroundings of the misplaced pieces, I was finally able to correct my mistakes and put them where they really belonged and construct a beautiful piece of art.

The puzzle (big picture) represents your purpose. While discovering your purpose, you may make some mistakes along the way. You'll find that you've placed certain people in positions they were never meant to occupy in your life. More than likely, you didn't fully evaluate their shapes, surroundings, intentions, personalities, etc. You took a quick glance and were deceived by the first impression. Some of us have encountered intimate connections with people that were only supposed to be a simple "hi & bye." Learn to know where people belong in your life. Some relationships have expired and should not be renewed nor repaired, and some should be restored. We tend to forget that while we're struggling with what we should do in life and in different situations, we have access to a whole guide that we subconsciously neglect; the Bible. Instead of referring back to the cover (Bible), we prolong processes by trying to figure it out by ourselves.

Trust in the Lord with all your heart and lean not on your own understanding. In all your ways acknowledge Him, and He shall direct your path. (Proverbs 3:5-6, NKJV)

Every move in your life should be strategic and intentional. No more "going with the flow," because you could very well be drifting down the wrong river. Learn and fulfill the assignment God has for you. After all, it's YOUR purpose that's on the line. The phone is ringing. Will you answer and complete the mission OR leave your work undone?

ARE YOU SCREAMING—HAVING A LIGHT BULB MOMENT like I was as I read this post? At this point, he and I began to dialogue back and forth.

I said, "Wait a minute—you just inspired me right in the middle of writing this chapter."

Sometimes as grown adults we struggle with certain

pieces of our lives. Some pieces are much broader than others. We try to discover where each piece belongs and fits, and we struggle even with the finished product—the "big picture"—on the cover of the box right in front of us.

What happens when you can't see the big picture—even when it's in front of you because you are gripped with fear, traumatized by pain, or in denial that something is broken that you can't fix?

I hear what others tell me, but for some reason, I can't comprehend the view of things getting better. Have you dropped a glass and the pieces around the edge shattered, but the base of the cup was still intact? You sweep up the pieces, then evaluate if the glass is worth saving. With glass, it's hard to put the pieces back together even with super glue. Because the container is no longer original, it's not a perfect fit. The broken pieces have rough edges, leaving gaps no matter how carefully you try to reconstruct the glass. And when any part of that glass shatters, putting it back together again may be impossible.

That's how life can be after a break, the edges of the situation and circumstances are ragged and rough. No matter how hard we try to reassemble our shattered heart, we may not be able to fit all the pieces back together.

But unlike a broken glass, our hearts are not disposable. We can't throw a heart in the trash and forget about it. Even if we have a hundred, a thousand or even a million pieces, we cannot leave our hearts shattered.

Is there hope for our broken hearts? How do we put so many pieces together again when we can't see the big picture and the colors and shapes just don't seem to fit?

We start with one simple step—picking up the pieces.

Chapter 4
Picking up the Pieces

Have you ever woke up and asked yourself, "How did I get here? What just happened?"

How do I take a day that was supposed to be normal when it suddenly becomes abnormal due to pain, tragedy and unexpected change? What was once solid is now shattered into a million pieces—at least it feels like a million pieces. And each piece is defined as some part of my life.

How do I define the person I used to be now that I'm living life through the eyes of disappointment and pain? Where is the "me" of yesterday?

One day, in an instant of a moment, divided into a second, my life changed forever. It was unexpected, unplanned, uninvited, unwanted, unbelievable and unbearable.

"It" is a two-letter word that has a particular definition in the lives of many people. *It* hurt me. *It* happened without my permission. *It* caused me to… I don't understand *"IT."*

It is the very situation and circumstance that invaded your life without permission. Was IT a death, divorce, breakup or wrong makeup, illness, betrayal, rape, or personal mistake? What was IT that caused your normal to become abnormal?

My function became dysfunction because of IT. I'm now tagged and identified by IT. Not by choice but by the thing that changed my normal world of living to abnormal.

When will the nightmare end? When will I feel freedom from pain and discomfort?

Unfortunately, that's going to take some work. Although "it" possibly happened without any warning, recovering from the shattering doesn't happen immediately.

How? I'm numb, yet angry because IT changed my perspective. IT took my power. My clear thoughts turned cloudy. My tender heart became rock solid. My smile dropped to a frown because of the thing or things I can't change.

All because IT changed me.

My calm spirit changed to chaotic. Day in, day out—I live in a fog of the unknown. Life dealt me a hand. And I just can't play that hand today.

IT shattered me, and I don't know how to put me back together.

Chapter 5
Living in the Moment

There's a saying that time heals all things. But what happens when your soul is wounded beyond repair?

Well, it feels that way when the pieces are all over the place after a break. It appears so easy just to put a Band-Aid on and dive into other things to ease the pain. However, just when you think you have come up for breath, there's another blow that hits you in your gut and knocks the wind out of you.

Have you ever experienced such deep pain that left you feeling as though you were drowning? Your head deep underwater, hands and arms swinging against the deep waves. All you see is the bottom of the pool.

You keep saying to yourself, "If I could just make it to the top, I could come up for air."

The funny part is you are stuck in the middle of this deep wave. You can't touch the bottom, and you can't reach the top. At least if you touch the bottom, you could use your feet to push you back up to the top. But somehow, the water is more of the enemy than the blow itself.

When I was a little girl, my mother enrolled me in swimming lessons at the local community swimming pool. I was so excited. She bought me a new swimsuit, swim cap and goggles. Set to go, I couldn't wait. On the first day, the swim cap came off, and I couldn't see out of the goggles.

From the opposite side of the swimming pool, the diving board hung in my view, summoning me from the shallow waters. I was so excited, ready to jump off that diving board. I wanted nothing more than to climb up there and jump into the cool, blue water—clueless about the depth.

The instructor told us to get in the water, hold on to the side of the pool. I was so anxious and excited to swim, wanting to go into the deep water without following the instructions of the instructor and at least learning the basics of swimming. I didn't like the lessons. They moved much too slowly in my opinion.

One lesson was how to hold my breath. How could I not know how to hold my breath? But I needed to learn the proper way to hold my breath underwater. There is a difference.

Have you ever been faced with a situation, and you feel as if you've been in it for so long? After a while, you just hold your breath waiting for the test to be over.

On the third day, I decided it might be a good idea to listen to the instructor and follow the instructions. I noticed the water grew darker the deeper it got, and it wasn't as easy to see in the deep as it was in the shallow water. So I stayed around the three-foot mark where I felt comfortable—where my feet still reached the bottom without my head going all the way under unless I wanted.

After about three weeks of learning the basics of swimming and passing my test to promote to the next level of the class, the instructor said, "Ok, now it's time."

Everyone in the class looked up with blank faces. "Time for what?"

He explained, "It's time to walk over to the diving board."

My heart sped up, beating so fast and hard I could barely breathe. All this time, I was anxious to JUMP, and at that moment the thought scared me.

Completely unexpected that day, he didn't prepare us ahead of time. I couldn't think it through. We all arrived to class expecting to do the same boring arm and leg exercises. And suddenly, wait a minute. This was not planned. Yet on the first day, I was anxious and excited. Jumping from the diving board was all I could think about. I looked across the pool daily, thinking what it would feel like to JUMP. When was the instructor going to tell us we could DIVE?

That particular day, he said it was time to put all of our basic lessons in action. At that moment, I couldn't remember whether to move my arms first or kick my feet. I wondered, "When do I hold my breath?"

So we climbed one by one up the ladder to get to the top of the diving board. OH LORD, I didn't realize we were JUMPING into the deepest part of the swimming pool. I shook all over. Looking at the side, I saw 12 FEET. No way.

As I approached the top, I kept hearing someone at the bottom scream, "Come on you can do it. You can do it."

Standing at the top of the diving board, looking down was the most frightening thing of my life up to that point. My daily instructor was at the top of the ladder with me, telling me what to do step-by-step. "Hold your breath and JUMP."

I cried. I didn't want to hold my breath and jump.

He said, "Be brave."

Immediately I responded. "It looked different from the other side of the pool. The diving board looked bigger, but standing here, it feels weak and not stable at all." I took a deep breath. "I'm scared because there's nothing to hold me. From a distance, it looks so easy, but now I'm here, I've changed my mind."

I definitely didn't want to jump anymore.

As I looked down, there were two other instructors waiting to catch me. They were not familiar to me. I only had this one instructor for the past three weeks. I couldn't trust them.

My instructor kept saying, "When you JUMP,

they'll be there to assist you. But you have to JUMP."

Terror filled my young body. I was holding up the line, and my fear became my class fear, spreading throughout the group. My fear caused everyone to be afraid.

Then finally the instructor said, "JUMP or you will have to go to the beginner's class and start over. You won't advance to the next class."

I stood there, shivering with thoughts coursing through my brain. Either I go back and start over or just go for it. So I JUMPED!

I hit the water, holding my nose. I fought the water with one hand and held my nose with the other.

The swim teacher below said, "Let go of your nose and hold your breath. Stop fighting me before you make both of us drown."

I released my nose and held my breath, just like I knew to do.

After I conquered that experience, I thought, "Oh that wasn't too terribly bad." But I wasn't trying to JUMP again anytime soon. One time was enough until I felt more comfortable swimming.

Today, I want to encourage you to JUMP. Just close your eyes and jump into your Life Purpose, realizing the very experience you encountered—the one that knocked the wind out of you—is turning into your Purpose.

Among my greatest joys is to talk with teen

mothers, comfort grieving mothers, or just sit and hold the hand of an elderly person who has no family. Why? Because I've been in each capacity. I've been a teen mom, scared silly without a clue about the future. I sat in the seat of a grief-stricken mother, trying to wrap my mind around how this happened to me. And now I'm taking care of my dad because my mom is deceased. Daddy has to make decisions all alone, which has given me a level of compassion for the elderly. When mother passed away, I had to jump in and help Daddy. When a family crisis comes up, I have to jump in and keep the family moving.

Jumping isn't easy, and it wears you down. So in the midst of your Jump, try something new. Find a new restaurant, try a new hairstyle, new hair color, or a new outfit that defines you. Come out of your comfort zone and do something bold. Ride a roller-coaster, visit a waterpark, try a new food or take a trip. Go for a massage or visit someone you haven't seen in years. Make this moment count or do something that puts a smile on someone's face.

Turning your Tragedy into Triumph can be very rewarding once you get to that place of freedom.

When I jumped off the diving board, my swimming coach and his assistant were in the water to catch me. Sometimes we just need someone to catch us when we fall. Don't stare at me. Don't ask how or why—just catch me.

Sometimes when we experience these tragic moments in our lives, we feel obligated to answer questions we have NO answers to. My grandpa, Mr. Esau Lewis, used to come visit us for the weekend. I enjoyed sitting and talking to him. Those were some of my fondest moments.

He would say, "Baby, sometimes there's just no answer to certain questions."

We often exhaust ourselves, trying to answer questions for people who really may not have our best interest at heart. Oh yes, it's true. Everyone in your circle might not always want to cheer you on or see you recover and be happy.

In recent years, I grew comfortable with loving me—satisfied in knowing I don't have to be everything to everybody. I learned the importance of being whole mentally, physically, emotionally and spiritually.

The greatest mistake we can ever make is trying to impress others. In a broken state, you will sometimes find out who your true friends are. It's sad to say it, but reality check... People can be in your life only for what that can or want to get out of you.

So many times we look at what others have, desiring to have their stuff and status. Truth be told, you don't know what they went through, or might currently be going through, to obtain what they have. It's easy to peek through the window, which can sometimes be deceiving until you walk through the actual door of a person's life.

Yes, they look nice driving that fine car. The bricks on the outside of their home speak wealth. Their children are dressed in fine designer clothes. From the outside looking in, you would classify their marriage as what you hoped for. However, you are only looking through the window. You have not stepped a foot inside the door to know what life experiences every day brings just to keep up an appearance.

What am I saying? Stop wishing you had what somebody else is fighting to HOLD ON TO. They may have the stuff, but you need to THANK GOD for your PEACE!

God gives us grace to handle what belongs to us. Stop stressing over what you see someone else with, and thank God for what He has graced you to carry.

Application Moment:

Today decide you will take on a new mindset, stop complaining and be thankful, stop comparing yourself to others. You will feel so much better. It starts with you loving yourself first.

Chapter 6
The Clean Up

Aftermath always follows a traumatic event.

Storms such as tornados, hurricanes and floods come at one time or another without any warnings. What was to be light rain or mist ended up being the type of storm that caused the most damage. In the aftermath, the things you once saw no longer exist, and the new reality doesn't look like the former. In a split second, everything you ever knew changed.

If things are not cleaned up properly, it can cause more damage and harm. After Hurricanes Katrina and Harvey, homes left standing were slowly destroyed by mold, bugs, and bacteria. People and things that had a home and a designated place to reside were now disrupted and displaced.

Have you ever experienced displaced anger? This is where you were angry and mad about something or at someone and you took it out on someone else. When life throws us an unexpected punch and we don't process through it in a healthy manner, it affects us. Trying to be strong and prove to people you can be happy and just move on, doesn't work. Smile while you are dying on the inside. You keep a straight, fake face in public, at work, at church, and around your family and friends. But you are shattered on the inside. The outward appearance looks good, but inwardly, the broken pieces keep cutting.

Often we tell everyone, "I'm fine. I'm ok. I'm over it." Many times we think it's true. But as time passes and seasons change, you find yourself in a situation where every little thing sets you off. You can't stand the voice of a person because it reminds you of something or someone. You dislike a person for no reason. Nothing satisfies you. From out of nowhere, you become judgmental, always finding yourself in the middle of chaos or drama.

Why?

Because you have not dealt with the aftermath of the previous storm in your life. You start a new relationship. Three months in, everything is peaches and cream. Then suddenly, he or she does something that reminds you of your past, and it sets you off. You start arguments because you are insecure. You pick a fight just for him or her to prove he or she loves you. This is all abnormal behavior. As you seek unhealthy attention in a broken area, you apply a Band-Aid for a temporary fix.

Timeout. Let's deal with the aftermath of your storm, which caused things in your life to be displaced, things in your emotions to be unstable.

Broken Trust is a dangerous thing, as we discussed earlier. If not totally dealt with and exposed, it will cause you to punish innocent people and subject them to an unhealthy relationship, causing them to compete with something fighting in you they cannot see.

Reality Check! You get out of one relationship that left you wounded. Or you stay in one that's a continuation day in and day out of either physical or mental abuse. It causes alterations to our behaviors, becoming someone we are not—and we know it. We develop seasonal internal cycles and patterns. One minute you're happy, the next minute you're miserable, causing others to suffer through misdirected anger. In reality, you can't fix them, and they can't fix you. The help has to come from inside of the person dealing with the broken trust, which shattered their emotional stability.

Application Moment:

Today, I will practice, the importance of being whole, mentally and emotionally. Today I will not lash out at others because I'm hurting from a wounded soul with scars from my past that has nothing to do with my current relationship or circumstance. Today I choose to be honest with myself. The person I see in the mirror will no longer be bitter but better. I choose to be happy, I choose to be free, and I choose to have peace in my inner being.

In a normal world, life is considered black and white. Unfortunately, some life circumstances and breaks cause you to experience that gray area where nothing makes sense. It's funny how people can portray you as superman or superwoman, thinking you are supposed to be super strong when faced with a crisis. Yes, we can be the strength for others, give advice, support, be good listeners, encourage and even pray for those friends or family members around us. But somehow, when it's your own personal life, you don't seem strong enough to help yourself. Nothing makes sense. Everything around you is falling apart. This is the point where you have to say it's ok not to be ok. The world will keep moving, so it's ok if you decide to be selfish and take care of yourself in that moment of need.

Are you one of those who tries to clean up other's mistakes, protect and cover up, just to keep the peace or to impress those around you? Well, I'm sorry to tell you, that's the worst thing you can do for the person, for yourself and for the situation.

Many times, we become a crutch for others in an unhealthy way. They continue to do what they want to do because they know you will always come to their rescue. As parents, we always want to protect our children. During my divorce from my younger girls' father, they were very young, still in elementary and middle school. I figured it was easier to just protect them and skip around questions they asked about their father and me. It was better for me to shield them from the truth. Guess what. That's not good. Remember they will not be babies forever, and eventually, they figure things out. You would rather them get the truth from you than create their own mental picture of what happened and caused them to battle with their emotions, blaming themselves, feeling guilty when it's nothing they did. It's better to be honest, and if the truth hurts them, they will understand as they get older.

I have talked with so many parents who experienced a divorce, and they wore themselves out trying to protect their children from the truth regarding the divorce. They cleaned up the mess of the other parent but didn't always do a good job. One or more of the children were still left with unanswered questions about why the other parent no longer lives in the home with them.

It is important to build a bond and relationship with your children, allowing them to ask questions, instead of them making assumptions. This helps them process their pain as well. Communication is the key to rebuilding life after a major life-changing event. It is very important to establish a line of communication with the parent living outside of the home for the sake of the children. There has to be some middle ground, where it's all about the children at this point. Like it or not, it isn't about two selfish, hurting adults, who at the moment may play the blame game, try to get the children on their side, and make the other parent seem at fault for everything.

While you struggle with your own emotions, you must remain true, yet not vindictive or pulling apart those stuck in the middle. Neither can you continually clean up after someone else or allow them to continually re-break the trust you extend.

As you recover from a broken trust, you may question many things, including what you thought to be true even about yourself. And that's where we're heading next.

Chapter 7
Shattered Identity

Sometimes we get to a crossroad in our lives where we have to make tough decisions. I married at a very young age the first time around. I was looking for love in all the wrong places instead of loving myself while finding my own identity. I thought my identity was tied to what someone else thought about me instead of believing in myself and having self-confidence in who I am. Even as a young girl all the way to my early twenties, I didn't know my full potential or my purpose in life. Instead, I saw it wrapped in an emotional relationship or the belief I had to be loved by a man to be validated. I convinced myself that was all I needed to form my identity.

When the first marriage didn't work out, I didn't seek my true identity. I kept going through life, thinking in order to be happy with myself, I had to be in a relationship. Growing up, I always dreamed of having a family, a house with the white picket fence, vacations, school programs, that solid rock marriage and living happily ever after. Well, that didn't happen. For one, my daddy spoiled me. On top of that, I was stubborn, although very loving and kind-hearted.

I expected marriage and family to look like what I grew up seeing through my parents. My daddy worked hard to provide, and yes, he was always at work, so my mother could stay at home.

Through the years, Mother said, "There's more to life than work. You have to invest time in your family and home. That job will always be there, but family may not. Life is too short."

Daddy always responded, "My job is to work and provide for y'all the ability to have what we need."

I watched my parents invest 45 years in marriage. Were they perfect? No—not at all. But they made it work, and they knew how to handle each other even when they didn't agree.

Sometimes I took sides and told Momma, "Tell daddy to hush!" What a joke.

At times, Mother was definitely upset with daddy for something or another he did or didn't do. Yet, my dad always spoke highly of my mother. He knew when she meant business. In her meek and humble character, she never raised her voice. But you better know when she got quiet, that was an indication she was serious and meant business.

As I got older, Mother taught me the true place of a lady. She talked to me many days about how a real lady carries herself. But as I matured, she demonstrated to me how a real lady never comes out of her character to prove anything to anyone. She modeled standing your ground with honesty, truth and prayer.

This was hard for me to exercise during that time in my life. While growing up, I had to have the last word. Remember, I'm the youngest, and I had brothers, so I had to prove to them I wasn't afraid of them at ALL.

Either as a senior in high school or just graduated in 1987, my dad and I got in the biggest quarrel because I wanted him to let me be an adult. He was trying to express to me otherwise, telling me I wasn't ready. According to him, I needed to decide on a school, travel the world, and not be anxious to jump out into this fast pace of life. He reassured me Mother and he would take care of Tori, my oldest daughter.

I didn't particularly want to hear his words, thinking I knew better than he did what was best for me. "Just get your education and prepare for your future, so you can take care of the both of you."

I can say my parents afforded me the opportunity to be all I could be. I was too afraid to leave home and them. I convinced myself they needed me, and they did. I laugh now as I look back at my stubbornness. While they might have needed me, I really needed them far more than they needed me.

Daddy and I bumped heads all the time because I wanted things my way. I yelled and cried.

Mother said, "That's still your daddy."

But I would be so mad at him. Right now I can't remember the specifics of why. All I remember is I wanted to be grown. I would go toe-to-toe with him in some form of debate.

He'd turn to my mother. "I know she's mad, and that's good because she's just like me. I want to make sure she don't let nobody run over her or take advantage."

Ohhhh—so he was provoking me.

He told my mom constantly, "I know what's in her. She's strong-willed, and she has the ability to go all the way in life."

Now, I didn't really know what that meant. During this time in life (in my early twenties), I still tried to please my parents, on one hand, and wanted them to be proud of me. But on the other hand, I couldn't figure me out. I worked hard to get the best jobs, nice cars, clothes, etc. "just to show them," determined that one mistake wouldn't keep me from making a life for myself.

I lost my identity in trying to please my parents and family and prove to them I could make it. Then I lost my identity trying to be all the strength in a relationship, which caused me to become dominating and overbearing (thank God for freedom). I had to take control, so I wouldn't be broken or battle depression because of what others did to hurt me.

As a reminder, I got married young for all the

wrong reasons, which caused much heartache. Then it got to the point, I was desperate for the relationship/marriage to work out. So I suppressed my thoughts and concerns, trying to keep the peace. Being the peacemaker is a good thing. However, make sure it's at the right time. Suppressing isn't healthy, and in the end, you will become a walking time bomb ready to explode at any given moment. This also increased anger issues I was already working through from my childhood.

My younger brother and I often got in fights when I was 8, and he was 12. So many times he laughed and held my head back while I swung my arms hitting nothing but air. Every once in a while he let me get in a few punches. Being the baby of the family can be a positive and a negative in some cases, and if you are the baby you know what I mean. My baby brother got on my nerves, but I loved him.

We encountered a few ups and downs growing up. I always covered up for him and told him where Mother hid the snacks on grocery day. As we got much older, we experienced some very hurtful things. Anger crawled all over me during those times. I worked hard at forgiving him, and it wasn't easy. Today we are closer and our relationship stronger.

I shared that to say for years, my identity made me feel like I had a problem with men and men had a problem with me, not understanding why relationships were always a strain. What had I done so awful to deserve such heartache and not be able to have a stable relationship? As time went on, I realized I have a great relationship with my brothers. My oldest brother and I have an unbreakable bond. Seeing that truth convinced me I didn't have a problem with men—at least not in general.

Growing up, I used to hate it when people identified me as my brother's little sister. Ugh—so annoying.

Usually, I responded, "No, it's me "Shawn." I have a name, and it's not Anthony and John's little sister."

On my first day of fourth grade, I was in the line ready to go into my math class, all excited about being in the fourth grade. The teacher came out of the room and saw me in line.

She asked, "Are you a Lewis?"

I paused. "Yes, ma'am."

"Who are your brothers?"

"Ma'am?"

She asked again. "Who are your brothers?"

Before I could respond, she said, "I know you are those Lewis boys' little sister."

I thought to myself, ok here we go. "Lady I have my own name and identity."

She called me the Lewis boys' little sister for the next three years. My entire time at that school when she saw me in the hall, that's how she identified me. Well, it ended up a good perk. She was very nice to me until I got in trouble for talking and had to stand outside the door. Then she threatened to call my mother but told me it wasn't necessary because my mother gave her permission to get ahold of my brothers.

Lord do I have to live in the shadow of my brothers? Why?

My siblings mean the world to me. We are closer now than ever. Much of that came from losing our mom and taking care of Daddy. But I don't want to live in theirs or anyone's shadows.

We have to understand, the problem is not always us. Sometimes certain people can't handle strong vessels. The strength of others intimidates them. But it's not the strong-willed person making them feel that way. The mindset and brokenness of the other person drive his or her apprehension.

I observed some things down through the years. Find a strong person with goals and ambition who works hard to build a future, stability, family-oriented values, saves money, and has big dreams. When that person believes in you, they push you to your next level. Then you can work together and build together, fortifying your future.

Listen, men—you don't have to be intimidated by a hard-working woman who is eager to get things done. As long as she stays in her lane, respects and honors you as the head of the relationship, be secure in knowing she has your back, and she loves you as her king.

Women, you don't have to be insecure in your role, nor intimidated in the stature of a hard-working man. Stop complaining if he desires to save for a season. If he says not right now, we are working toward having something of our own—such as owning a home, paying off debt, or building a business and future for the family—be secure and trust him. As long as you can see the fruit, then be ok with accepting the fact you don't have to keep up with the Jones' next door to prove anything to anyone. Just be patient and true to yourself and him and watch the progress.

After many years of trial and error, I discovered my identity was the relationship. NOPE! That's not what made me who I was or desired to be.

My identity was ME.

When things got rocky in both my marriages, in friendships, or with jealous co-workers. I would always take the low road and blame. It's my fault. What can I do better, and how can I fix me to their liking? We as women have to come into the knowledge of understanding you can't fix someone who's already broken. We of the female species want to be Ms. Fix IT, thinking they will love you for what you do and not for who you are.

Buying love and acceptance is not the answer. Make sure your motive of what and why you are doing it is pure and for all the right reasons. If you sat and talked over nothing but a coke and some potato chips, that should be enough as long as you have each other. So there you already put your identity in the relationship instead of knowing who you are before you GO ALL IN.

Application Moment:

Repeat after me, I can't be to others what I'm not to myself. I can't help them until I can help me. There are things beyond my control. However, I will not allow those things to control who I am. I take back my self-esteem, my self-confidence and most of all, I take back everything that robbed me of my peace. I love me, and today that's enough. I will no longer allow the insecurity of others to exhaust me. Today I declare, I'm free!

On April 16, 2002, after the death of my mother, I lost my identity as a daughter. I'm a daughter without a mother. Mother's Day was the first holiday without her, and it was so hard for me and my entire family. All the commercials made me angry. Going to our family church was difficult because she was always there when the doors opened. Not being able to see her put a hole in my soul.

The earth-shattering morning when my dad called to tell me she passed out and he couldn't get her to wake up was one of the worse days of my life. For some reason that particular morning, I was fully dressed and ready to walk out the door.

I said, "Wait. Why didn't I brush my teeth? I walked back to the bathroom, brushed my teeth, and came out to the phone ringing—around 7:15 a.m. My strong daddy's voice sounded frail and frightened as his unbelievable words came through the line.

Weeks prior to that morning I had a dream about my sister and me riding in a terrible storm. In the dream, I drove this big SUV. The wind raged and the rain hit so hard I couldn't see the road in front of me. I woke up crying and hysterical. I got the phone, went into the bathroom at 3:00 a.m. and called Mother. She answered just as jolly as ever. Yes, she was awake. I couldn't get a word out, crying so hard.

She said, "You must have had a dream."

I sobbed into the phone, still unable to speak.

Her soothing voice came across, calming and peaceful. "Was it your daddy, or was it me?"

I cried and told her about the storm where I was driving but couldn't see. In my dream, we made it to our destination out in East Texas, and Mother came out of this house and said, "I'm tired."

It wasn't what she said. It's how she said it that crushed my soul.

The day mother died, a brutal storm hit the metroplex. Within an hour, one part of town was ripped to pieces. It thundered, flooded in some areas, and a tornado was reported to have touched down on the southeast side of Fort Worth. It didn't register until later after the sun came out and storms passed over, leaving an aftermath of damage. Sometimes God will use dreams, people, or odd situations to prepare us in an unusual way. Although we may not recognize it at that very moment, there are small indications that something is different. We don't replay it until afterward. As we talk things out, you realize and pinpoint different scenarios and put moments together like the center of a puzzle.

The day before mother passed, she called to let me know she would be out running a few errands. I needed to stop by but figured I would circle back because I also had errands. On any normal given day, my girls would be with Mother as she was babysitting—especially MaKayla. She spent many days with Mother, going with her to church, visiting family and friends, and grocery shopping.

When I would pick her up after work, she would say, "I stay with Grandma."

Mother loved the company. Another instance of that day being different, MaKayla wasn't there because I made her come home. Things like that played in my mind. I was angry with myself for not circling back like I said I would. That was the last time I heard her voice—April 15, 2002, around 2:30 p.m.

Life has a way of dealing you a hand you refuse to

play.

So many emotions exploded after my mother passed away. I tried going to counseling, but that didn't work. It started out ok, but it was getting hard, and I was uncomfortable. With counseling, you might go in for one issue, but other issues must come up to get to the root of the issue at hand.

Then you ask yourself, "What does one issue have to do with the other?"

At that point, compacted issues lay buried under each other. You can't get to one without digging up the other. Sounds crazy, doesn't it? Well, that's how the mind and emotional part of the human body works. When there has been trauma to a part of your body, emotional and mental state, you have to deal with all of it in order for healing to take place. The bleeding and wounds have to be assessed and a plan of action for your recovery all has to be evaluated so you gain the best recovery in a healthy manner.

There's not a day goes by that I don't miss my mother. She taught me the true meaning of faith. However, I had to walk out the words she taught me in real life situations. I could not wrap my mind around her death. Why would God allow Mother to pass at such an early age of 58? The younger girls will never know Grandma. MaKayla has a small memory of her, but Jaslin has no memory of my mother at all. She was very little when Mother passed away.

This was another identity crisis for me as well. I needed my mother to help me be a better mother in this stage and season of my life. I was no longer the teen mom. I was a married mom, needing her mother. This was a very difficult time for my entire family. Holidays were hell!

Our first Christmas without mother, my sister, brothers and I literally got up in her bed and cried, sobbed and cried some more, missing her dearly. The house didn't smell like Christmas. There were no decorations, and we totally skipped Thanksgiving. How could this be? We still needed our mother.

Her death and the holidays following began a spiral of heart-wrenching events. Once we got through the holidays, we started trying to pick up the pieces. What was supposed to get easier, as people stated, got worse. Friends and family returned home, the phone stopped ringing, cards stopped coming, and the funeral home picked up all the chairs. What's next? None of us knew.

One song, "My Soul Has Been Anchored" by Douglas Miller, resonated in my heart for months. Now mind you, at that point, I was yet angry with God. He had so many other people He could have taken. Why mother? This song kept coming to me for months. I didn't want the storms, even with an anchored soul. I wanted Mother. But the song reminded me I did have an anchor, and He held me firm.

Application Moment:

If you feel you have **Lost Your Identity** *while navigating through a life crisis, this is a great time to take a moment a do a self-evaluation. Ask yourself, when did I stop believing in me? Why did I stop believing in me? Repeat these words aloud as you read. I <u>(Your Name)</u> take back my identity that was stolen or given up during the time I was <u>fill in the blank </u>(raped, abused, betrayed, sick, etc.) Today I rediscover who I am mentally and emotionally. I will no longer be a prisoner or hostage of my personal demons that haunt me. I will no longer be tormented by the person or people who invaded my life with hurt, pain and disappointment. I'm encouraged to push past and through each day with a heart of gratitude, knowing I survived. I will not stop living, I will not just exist in the shadow of my pain, but I will live every day as an overcomer. I forgive all who afflicted pain in my life. I take back my authority for being the person God ordained me to be. I'm not only surviving, but I'm thriving in the joyful harmony of life.*

"I look up to the mountains – does my help come from there? My help comes from the Lord, who made heaven and earth!" (Psalm 121:1-2, NLT)

And may I interject right here? And God created "YOU and ME." We are His creation, and He knows just when we need Him the most. He knows how much we can bear. I don't say that lightly.

Chapter 8
Forgiveness is the Key

Modern technology designed a way that you don't need a key to unlock the front door—a new way to unlock doors using a digital keypad. However, I'm an old-fashioned girl, and I still like to use my key.

Ask me why?

Well, I'm glad you asked. I like to use the old-fashioned method of unlocking the front door. For one, you know the key is going to work. With digital keypads, they can stop working at any moment. You have to replace the battery often. If you decode it by entering the wrong code more than once, you risk not being able to lock or unlock the door.

What does a digital keypad have to do with forgiveness? Focus on the key. You hold the original key to unlock the door. Imagine standing before a door, wanting inside so badly because outside is cold and scary. Suddenly, you realize you have a key, and it fits the lock. You're inside as soon as you turn it. You have that key to open forgiveness.

The first key of forgiveness partially opens the lock

and starts with forgiving yourself for whatever happened, not looking for others to blame or retaliate against and injure because you hurt. Next, the key to acceptance admits something happened to change your life. Then the key to understanding assures you it is ok not to understand. This key tends to stick as we search with that question of why. Sometimes you can't understand what happened, so you keep replaying things over and over and over. Yet still, there's no reason to the mad matter.

Allowing your heart to forgive, even when you know others did you wrong, remember you have the power to overcome. We so often kill ourselves trying to figure out what the person who hurt us is thinking and why are they thinking so negatively toward us to hurt us.

Funny logic in our trying to figure this out. For example, a married couple doesn't just fall out of love. 99% of the time, the person inflicting the pain is still in love with the person they hurt. Their acts of unkindness cause wounds in spite of love. I used to ask myself why love hurts so badly. The word "love" is supposed to live up to its meaning. I finally figured out it's not the word's fault, nor is it the word "love" causing pain. It's actually the person you love who causes the pain and damages the relationship.

I learned a long time ago, you can't tell your heart who to love. That's the function of the heart. It captivates that to which it is attracted or to which the heartstrings attached themselves.

Amazingly, a pregnant mom falls in love with a baby she has not yet seen. Her love grows stronger while she carries the baby in her womb. She nurtures, feeds and talks to an unborn baby she hasn't laid eyes on, yet she's in love with this little human being long before he or she enters the world. But the child already makes this great imprint in the heart of the one carrying him or her.

The same goes for adults. Have you heard the saying "love at first sight?" You fall in love with a person you meet for the first time. How could that be? Simple—your heart was captivated by looks, voice, mannerism, materialistic status, money, or for a dozen other reasons. Loving someone comes naturally to us. Unfortunately, the one whom you love dearly will do something to hurt you and betray the love—just as you are capable of hurting someone who loves you dearly, and both hearts and emotions have made a long- or short-term investment. You ask yourself, "Did I just waste my time?" The answer to that question only you can answer. But we can't let even the deepest agony leave unforgiveness in our lives.

Unforgiveness is the root cause of misery. It controls, is unruly, and has no understanding. When a person allows unforgiveness in his or her heart, he or she is a walking time bomb, ready to explode at any given moment.

I picture unforgiveness as this big brick sitting in the middle of a person's heart and a trash bag over the person's brain. I know that sounds funny. A trash bag? Yes, a big black trash bag that caused bitterness within the perception of the person who harbors unforgiveness. I can say this because this is how I felt when I carried unforgiveness in my heart toward people and circumstances I couldn't control or keep from hurting me.

A situation I faced in the past overwhelmed me. I loved and trusted some people. But again, what does love have to do with it? When people's minds are made up to do what they want regardless of the impact on others, there's nothing you can do about it.

One day, I heard this still, small voice say, "Let it go. You are going to kill yourself, stressing out over what someone has done, that you couldn't accept or deal with. No, it may not be fair, but that's on them and not on you."

Innocent people get hurt all the time, but I was angry because that wasn't supposed to be me. You figure you try to do good in the world, and still there's no control of what others do to bring harm on someone else.

I know you've heard this many times—when you don't forgive someone, you give them the power to control your emotions. That's really a true statement because you are forever locked into the mindset of asking yourself why? Wondering if things had gone this way or that way. What if there's never an answer to why a person's actions toward you never make any logical sense?

Have you ever thought that might just be part of the plan?

I know that sounds crazy. But what if the very thing God allowed someone to do to break you fits within His plan?

Notice I said allow. Chances are, that event was part of your making. It was part of your testimony. It was part of your learning to trust God at a deeper level. The situation perhaps helped you build a business, building your character and integrity. It showed you how not to do others. And it enlightened you to have a deeper level of compassion.

Sometimes, if we take the time to think through what we experienced and allow that to ignite us to do something different, we will be a greater influence in this world. If I never experienced worrying about paying bills as a single mom, I would never be able to relate to single mothers and their daily issues. If I never experienced the loss of my mother, I could never understand a child of any age missing his or her mom. If I had never been without a job, I would never feel the heart of someone looking for work, qualified for many jobs but finding no one will hire them. If I never experienced financial hardship, there's no way I could write and say, "I understand."

Oh, I do understand. We have to be careful not to fall in the pit of self-righteousness, looking down on others and questioning why they are going through something hard or what they did.

Most likely, they did nothing! Neither did we do anything. Sometimes it's simply because that was part of the plan.

Application Moment:

Repeat after me. Life curve balls are part of my purpose and the plan of God. Today, I forgive myself. I will no longer hold myself hostage in unforgiveness. I choose to let go and HIT the reset button. I recalibrate my thoughts not to focus on the person or people who hurt me. I choose to release them in love. Jesus Christ forgives us so many times and yet has mercy on us when we do wrong. Today, I choose unconditional love moving forward. Pain with a Purpose.

Chapter 9
Financial Break (Hardship)

Financial hardship may be caused by either a decrease in income or unforeseen increases in expenses. Some reasons for hardship include losing your job, a reduction in overtime, not being able to work due to medical reasons, large medical expenses, unexpected car or house repairs, and/or the loss of spousal income due to death.

No matter how well you manage your expenses based on your income, life can throw a curve ball that derails your financial plans. And often those curve balls come in rapid succession.

When you face financial hardship, it may seem like your only option is to choose which bills you can afford to pay month-to-month, at least until you find a way to make ends meet. My personal experience as a single mother made me feel humiliated and all alone. I was ashamed, feeling I had nowhere to turn. I didn't know how to seek out resources to educate me with the necessary actions to help with high-cost medical bills. Even with the best of medical insurance, there were copays for doctor's visits, balances on hospital stays as well as prescriptions that cost more than my utility bills.

If you find yourself in financial hardship, don't be ashamed. Allow people to help you meet financial obligations and preserve your personal credit—even when your income takes a hit due to circumstances beyond your control. Ask for help! Connect with a social worker and agencies that can point you in the right direction.

Statistics show that men and women of all different races and nationalities have committed suicide due to the pressure of a financial obligation they could no longer meet. Under many different financial circumstances, the pressure mounts. Yes, in some cases we make bad decisions, which contributes to the hardship when unexpected events pop up. Even then, don't allow this to take a heavy toll on your life.

I was in denial, thinking everything would get better. But better didn't come for a very long time. Saving for emergencies, if you can, is critical. Avoid it, and the worst thing you can do is continue to dig deeper in debt by taking loans you can't afford to pay back. Eventually, you find yourself looking up from a dark hole. At the time, I felt the only way out came in the form of a Pay Day Loan. Huge mistake. Before I knew it, my entire paycheck was compromised each week.

My dad afforded us the opportunity as teenagers to

visit the bank and open a savings account. He taught us how to write a check with the understanding you must have funds in the account to make the check good.

There's a saying that all I need is a million and my life will be complete. Well, money does make life a little easier in some instances, but I beg to differ that it brings complete peace or happiness in life. Why do I say that? When my daughter was in the hospital, I had just received my tax return. I had money in the bank, but it wasn't enough to make her well. I was miserable and frustrated. Fast forward to the year after her death. Bills piled up like a mountain. I had to get a CPA to help with my taxes. I filed for a hardship withdrawal from my 401K.

Now if I had millions in my bank account, there would not have been the worry of rushing back to work or trying to figure out how to take care of two little girls. So yes, finances are very necessary to take care of living expenses. The important point here is not allowing money to control us. Save for the unexpected, prepare for rainy days. Financial breaks and hardships contribute to stress, heart attacks, and divorce.

My financial hardship was a very difficult time in my life. Maybe you experienced a layoff or decline in your savings for whatever reason. God is a God of another chance. Take your negative experiences and use them as a stepping stone to a life of humility and wisdom, gratitude and service.

I shared before that even during my hardship, I was committed to paying my tithes. Many thought I was crazy for doing so. But today, I know God remembered me because I remained faithful in the small things. During my financial drought, He remembered my tenth and first-fruits with which I honored Him. Yes, I faced some difficult times with no gas or food and utilities being cut off, just to keep my head above water while I was sinking. God gave Job double after he lost everything. He did the same for me, and God can and will restore you after the storm.

The goal is to find solutions that empower you to reestablish your financial footing and get back on the right track. There are programs designed to provide temporary financial relief so you can maintain your financial obligations until your situation improves.

Again, **you're not in this alone**. Be proactive before things spiral out of control.

Application Moment:

I set my pride aside, seeking to do what's best for my family. This is not the time to be selfish and continue to spend and be wasteful. If it's not necessary, I don't purchase it. Remember this situation is only temporary.

"If God is for us, who can be against us? Who shall separate us from the love of Christ? Shall tribulation, or distress, or persecution, or famine, or nakedness, or danger, or sword? No, in all these things we are more than conquerors *through him who loved us. For I am sure that neither death nor life, nor angels nor rulers, nor things present nor things to come, nor powers, nor height nor depth, nor anything else in all creation, will be able to separate us from the love of God in Christ Jesus our Lord." (Romans 8:31-39 ESV, selected)*

Chapter 10
The Mental Break

This is an intensely sensitive area for me. Have you ever been in a place where you couldn't hold your thoughts together? Where nothing made sense to you anymore? Your brain was in a fog. You woke up, but your brain didn't wake up with you.

I experienced depression during a very hard time in my life, and I can be honest—it happened on multiple occasions. After remembering these times, then I had to accept the fact it started as a teenager.

I was in a really cold place in my life, finding out I was pregnant. My parents wanted the best for me, and as they saw things changing, they were upset. Their little girl becoming a teen mom certainly didn't fit their plans for my best. I hid the fact that something was changing in my body, but I didn't know how to tell my mom. Signs of something different were obviously there. I threw up at the smell of McDonald's—always tired, sleepy. But who would have thought pregnant? Not me.

The big question came. I called my mom to pick me

up from school.

She said, "Yes, I will be there, and we need to talk."

I thought to myself, ohhhhh this is not good. "We need to talk" with a serious tone seldom leads to something good.

She picked me up, and on the ride home she said, "Someone noticed that your waistline has changed."

Now mind you, she lived in the house with me, and I believe she noticed but was in just as much denial as I was. I remained active, playing volleyball, running track.

No. Can't be—not possible.

When we got home, she had a pregnancy test waiting on me. I stood in that bathroom for what seemed like an eternity, trying to figure out if I really wanted to face this place in life. During this time, my dad was ill and off work. My mother was a stay-at-home mom, which I loved. How could I put this pressure and worry on them, while so many things were unraveling before us?

Mom's voice boomed through the bathroom door. "Hurry up. You should be finished."

I ran the water and flushed the toilet. How was I going to face this? I knew what caused pregnancy, and I was guilty. But I couldn't be pregnant. Still, I took the test, left it in the bathroom, and went and sat on the porch.

Mother called me back in the house. "Well, you're

pregnant, and we are going to the doctor in the morning."

For me, a weight lifted off my shoulders. "Well now, at least I know what's wrong with me." I laughed, trying to lighten the mood.

She cried. I cried. Then she put her hand on my cheek and reassured me all would be ok.

This is the part that's so hard for me to expose, but it's necessary. As my mother asked about the father, she knew at the time I only liked one person—my first love.

I told my mother half the truth, which was still a lie.

"Mom, I was raped."

In my mind, I wasn't lying completely. I had been raped, but I never told her about the incident. It happened years prior, then the molestation, which occurred when we went to visit some particular friends. I saw a way of escape, telling her, "Mom, something happened to me. I couldn't tell you then, but I'm' telling you now." I thought this would keep her from being disappointed and angry with me and my first love. I didn't want her to be mad at either of us.

The truth of the matter, this conception was due to love. Although we were young, naive, and immature, a beautiful life was conceived. That was the good part of the deal—that beautiful, innocent life.

Mother took me to the doctor who confirmed the at-home test. I was nearly six months pregnant. We left the doctor, got lunch, and she dropped me off at school. I played my last volleyball game of the season. And guess what. I gave it everything I had. Over the next few months, things changed drastically.

Now that everyone knew about the pregnancy, I began to suffer depression really bad. I cried all the time because my new normal was majorly different. I couldn't express to my mother how difficult it was. I already made a mess of things, so I didn't want to make things worse. She became more protective of me, and I began to isolate myself.

My thoughts outweighed my heart, which was already broken. My relationships with friends changed. Every day, I struggled, trying to hold it together.

Day in and day out I wondered, "What's the use of being on this earth?"

I wanted the pain in my brain to GO AWAY! I was mad at myself, confused, and constantly in tears. I contemplated several things I could do to bring this pain to an end. I just wanted to stop hurting. Being young and in love compacted these emotions as well.

One night I said, "This is it."

I went to the bathroom and took a bottle from the medicine cabinet. I stared at the blue pills for a while. Then I closed my eyes and consumed them.

All I wanted to do was sleep—forget about life and all of my problems for a while. Every waking moment meant thinking about the life in me and how badly I messed up. If I could just sleep…

I went back to bed, laid there for a minute, and thought, "How selfish of you. You have a little life inside of you. Why would you do this?"

Weakness drifted over my body, deep and unrelenting. So I got up enough strength to walk to my parents' bedroom, knocked on the door and roused Mom.

"I need to go to the hospital."

Mom shot up in the bed. "Why? What's wrong? You look funny." She got up. "What's wrong with the baby? Are you in pain?"

So many questions firing in my direction. "No. I took some pills that were in the medicine cabinet."

Mom rushed into the bathroom to see what they were. Without saying a word, she put me in the car and took me to the ER.

In the car, I hung my head and spoke quietly. "I'm so sorry for all the pain I caused, Mom. I'm tired of my brain hurting, I'm tired of thinking, and I'm tired of issues replaying over and over in my mind. I just wanted to stop the pain."

We got to the hospital. They rushed me in the back. Mom told the doctor I was pregnant and took a bottle of pills. Their main focus was on making sure the baby was ok. My main focus centered on my mental head to stop hurting and my thoughts to stop haunting me.

The nurse came in asking all types of questions.

Once they got me settled, she asked, "Are you

depressed?"

I didn't know how to answer because I didn't know what depression was. I shrugged.

She said, "You just tried to harm yourself and your unborn baby."

I thought about it for a moment. "I never wanted to bring harm to my baby. I just wanted for my brain to stop aching."

I didn't know how to tell the nurse more than that. How did I explain that I wanted visions of things I suppressed years prior and couldn't tell anyone about to go away? Why now has this all come up? Perhaps because I was still and couldn't move around, come and go as I did before I was pregnant. All I had was time to think. And those thoughts became my enemy. I didn't want to intentionally hurt my baby, but my brain ran on overload. Piercing thoughts constantly cut my heart wide open. My heart and soul cried out for help, but nothing came out of my mouth.

The doctor ran tests and came to the critical moment to see if the baby still had a heartbeat.

He asked, "Have you felt the baby move?"

"Not really." I wasn't sure what a baby moving around inside felt like, to be honest.

He continued with the exam while the nurse held my hand. The doctor took the little handheld Doppler and placed it on my belly. It seemed everyone in the room held their breath. After a few minutes, the corners of his mouth moved up a bit, and then a big smile spread across his face.

"Do you want to hear your baby's heartbeat?"

Tears broke loose and streamed down my face uncontrollably. "No," I said. "That's too hard."

"No. It will make you feel better." He turned up the volume on the sonogram machine.

At first, strange sounds came from the speakers, but then a distinctive thumping overshadowed all the other sounds. For the first time, I heard the heartbeat.

The doctor said, "This little one is a trooper."

The nurse sat by my side, still holding my hand. "You know what? You are not the only teen mom. You can take this experience and make something great for you and your child." She squeezed gently. "Take what you think is a failure and turn it into possibilities. Once you lay eyes on this sweet life, you will immediately fall in love—I promise."

I couldn't say anything, my voice choked by the tears. But they didn't stop my thoughts.

Why would this little life need me? I can't help myself at this moment. I'm too shattered and broken to give him or her the love it deserves.

My mom came into the room. "Today is a new day. We are going to make it through this."

Finally, she realized I was in pain for more than one reason or another, and it wasn't physical pain. My pummeled mind screamed in excruciation.

The good news came a couple of months later when I gave birth to a beautiful, healthy baby girl with no issues from the pills.

I took the nurse's advice, left there and said, "I have to make the best of this."

While I waited for my daughter's arrival, I set goals and made plans for my life. I resolved to do something to make my parents proud of me, and most of all be a good mother.

On January 24, 1985, I was admitted to the hospital, having labor pains and thinking surely I was going to die. That cold and rainy day came after a night of sleeplessness when I walked the kitchen floor, wondering how anything could hurt so much.

My mother simply said, "You are in labor."

Funny, she took her time taking me to the hospital. Once we made it there, they took me to a nice private room, which I know many young teens don't get to experience. This time was very pivotal for me, causing me to think, mature, and make decisions in a heartbeat. At the end of delivering my first child, I became a woman and mother.

One moment still engraved in my mind is the cold delivery room. Back then they wheeled you to a different room when you were ready to deliver.

That was the most frightening moment, and I kept saying to myself repeatedly, "I will never be back here again until I'm good and ready." I prayed so hard, asking God to help me.

At the moment of Tori's birth, I made up in my mind. I resolved to make something of my life, to make my parents proud. That was extremely hard because I was so young and still wanted to experience life as a teen and young adult.

As a single teen parent, I faced a great adjustment, but I had wonderful help from my parents and awesome support from family. During this critical time in my life, I was so very young and had no clue what parenting was all about. I was afraid and didn't know what to expect. A major moment in my life, I felt so confused and all alone, feeling I disappointed my family. I became what I said I wasn't going to be—part of the statistics of teen moms, young and inexperienced, unwed, no job, and having the responsibility of another life.

My mother was my rock during those times. She prayed with me and for me and encouraged me to be the best woman and mother possible. She taught me many things through this process, and even today I'm forever grateful.

Each of us, with all of our triumphs and failures, joys and heartbreaks, scars and all, have been given an opportunity to make a difference in the world. Do not underestimate what God can do with a life solely surrendered to Him. Give God all the broken pieces. For who knows if you are where you are today "for such a time as this?" (See Esther 4:14)

Breakthrough in My Brokenness
Written By Crystal Kelley (used with permission)

I see now that you had me in the fire, with a purpose like Jeremiah
For in my mother's womb you shaped me with destiny and a desire
A desire to speak to nations, seek your truth with wisdom and revelation
And through your Word offer the joy of your salvation
So through the years and tears, the joys and the fears
You placed strength in me I didn't realize I had to help me persevere
Father, can you make it clear? My "there" is now here
I've been chosen and considered for such a time as this
Yet, I need you to restore me; heal me in spite of my brokenness
This test came with some lessons perhaps I couldn't study for
However, this has only brought me to a place of dwelling on your threshing floor
And now I need you more and more; possibly more than the day before
When I thought I was losing this race, you stepped in my place to even the score
If it's not one thing, it's another; tried to stay under the covers
For a split second, I thought you didn't care until you reminded me that we were lovers
You love me where I am while loving me to where I am going to be
You changed up the recipe so I wouldn't give up on the road to destiny
You're the God who specializes in storms that get worse
You're the only one I know who can speak to the waves and command them to reverse

Shattered Pieces: Broken2Blessed

Lord, quench my thirst; no better yet, keep me longing for your water
If everything was 100, there would be no need to stay on the altar
When I began to falter, Lord please keep me on the straight and narrow
I must keep pressing; draw me back like a bow to an arrow
Continue watching over me like your eye is on the sparrow
I no longer desire to stay in Egypt; give me the boldness to speak to Pharaoh
Your Word says if I abide in You, in me You will abide
But sometimes, I can barely eat the main entrée let alone the sides
Entangled in a web, like my issues have gone worldwide
I thought I had the combination to the lock but my access was denied
Like Jacob, I'm walking this one out but holding on to my hip
"Angel, I won't let you go even if it means tightening up my grip!"
My tears began to drip because to You they are prophetic
Wherever you go I'll follow; wow, now that's magnetic
It might be hectic, might feel neglected, but for you, I've been elected
It was unexpected, might be rejected, but my life is Christ's; therefore, it is reflected
I'm steadfast to your promise; it's in your word that I hide
When you're ready to turn this track over, Lord I know you'll "show me the flipside"!

Broken Whole
©2011 A Peace of Crystal Vol. 1

Chapter 11
The Enemy of the Mind

Being angry is a terrible state to be in. Everything and everybody is a moving target.

As years went by, being this young mother, working hard, frustrated, impatient, tired all the time and still trying to find me, was a very difficult season in my life. Not much more than a child myself, I had no wisdom and often felt like I was missing out on something in life.

The older my daughter got the more we argued all the time.

My mother told me, "You have to learn how to talk."

"I am talking," I argued back.

"No, you are fussing, and when you are fussing and screaming, nobody wants to listen."

"No, Mother. That's not what that is."

We had this same conversation many times. Then she asked me one day, "What are you so angry about?"

"I'm not angry, Mother. That's just the way I express myself."

"No. That's anger." I didn't want to hear that from my mom, but it made me think.

I began to monitor and watch my response to certain things, especially with my daughter. At this time I was around 24 and my daughter Sha'Toriya (Tori) was blooming into this beautiful young lady. She was smart, bright and very intelligent.

We were riding in the car one day and she said, "Momma, I have a boyfriend."

Mind you she was still in elementary school—still a baby in my mind. I almost ran off the road.

I started screaming to the top of my lungs, losing it.

Tori laughed. "I don't have a boyfriend. I just wanted to see what you would say and your response."

Instead of stopping, calming down, I kept going on and on and on, giving her all these lectures, telling her she's not going to make the same mistakes, I made, so forth and so on.

She responded, "Mom, please stop."

Well, there was another outburst of anger I didn't know was living on the inside of me. My mind went straight to all the things I encountered and didn't want her to experience—all those hurts and pains. So I went from 10 to 10,000! Instead of calmly talking, I yelled. I inflicted her with my wounded heart and the anger buried deep inside of me.

I was angry with myself, for not speaking up when I was molested. I was angry because of friends that betrayed me. I was angry because I was in a hard place, and I didn't want to be. And mostly, I was angry because my thoughts never rested. I exploded like a time bomb when it wasn't necessary—all over a silly little joke.

We so often take our anger issues out on innocent people. The saying **"Hurt People – Hurt People"** is very true. We make innocent people suffer from things that happened to us in the past. Most of the time they have no knowledge of what we went through, but we leave them cut and bleeding in the wake of our own unresolved pain. We don't mean to do it, but from our depths, anger spills out and wounds those closest to us.

Being angry comes from a spirit that consumes your ability to reason things through. There's a scripture in the Bible that reads, *"Don't sin by letting anger control you, don't let the sun go down while you are still angry (meaning don't end your day mad). This gives a doorway for the devil to reside in your mental capacity (enemy of the mind) to rule and sabotage your thoughts"* (Ephesians 4:26, NLT).

At one time in my life, my mind was in prison, locked up in all the things consuming me. One day while driving down the freeway, 820 west to be exact, I looked up. I had passed my exit. I couldn't remember what exit to get off on. My mind literally went blank.

I kept asking myself, "Where are you going? Where are you going?"

It was like I was sleep driving. I finally snapped out of the stupor and remembered I was to go around the ramp to I35 south. By this time, I was near Hulen Mall.

For a minute I asked myself, "Is this what happens when a person's mind snaps and leaves them?"

That was a horrible feeling. I tried to hold on to my thoughts. Of course, at that time, I had more things going on than just my mother's death. My marriage was strained, I had small children and my oldest wasn't feeling well. I constantly had a hard time concentrating at work. I was tired of people telling me to get over it and move forward. A snowball of emotions rolled over me, and my mind literally shut down. It was a very discouraging time.

I did my best to make it from one day to the next—or more like one second to the next. I can recall getting into my car, driving through my neighborhood crying, telling my mom I couldn't do this without her. I prayed, "Lord, help me, or I'm not going to make it." I was in a serious place of desperation.

One day the phone rang. I answered, and on the other end heard Trinia James. I deeply admired her and drew encouragement from her ministry. With holidays approaching, she knew it would be a hard time for my family and me.

She expressed her concern. "I'm just calling to check on you."

I responded short and immediately tried to get off

the phone.

She said, "Wait a minute. I'm in town and wanted to stop by to see you."

"I don't think so. I'm not feeling well, Trinia."

"I just want to see you, give you a hug, and then I'll leave."

There I was grieving, so angry I wanted to be left alone. I stayed on the couch the entire week after Christmas, no cooking dinner or anything. I can't remember what my children ate because I was in such a bad state of mind.

A couple of months prior to Mother's passing, Trinia came to town for a revival and a women's gathering. She stayed with my mother. During her visit, she actually planned to stay at the hotel. But Mother invited her to come home with her and visit after the women's fellowship. The next morning, Trinia was the speaker at our church, and she rode in with Mother.

After the visit, Mother spoke so fondly of her, how they enjoyed talking and the wisdom Mother shared with her that created an immediate bond. When she got word that Mother passed away, she immediately came to be with me. She didn't say much. She was just with me, which meant very much. After the funeral, Trinia returned home to East Texas but kept in touch. Maybe she sensed my pain or heard something in my voice, but she didn't accept any excuses from me.

That day, I finally agreed to her coming over, and to

my surprise, she knew I was in this funk.

She said, "If you don't mind, I'm going to sit right here." She sat on the floor beside the couch. "I'm not going to say anything if you don't want me to. I'm just going to sit here."

I got very upset with her because I wanted to be left alone, not realizing I was experiencing a delayed grief burst as well as depression.

My sink was piled with dishes, the laundry on one end of the couch and me on the other with my head buried under a blanket. Trinia spoke few words for about an hour, but then she started with small words that finally produced questions. Then large sentences broke out. She convinced me to eat something. Of course, the fridge was empty, so she sent her husband out to get some food.

You know, it's amazing how she maneuvered her way into my world of seclusion and got me to talk.

Finally, she said, "Your babies need their momma."

I looked at her, feeling a frown on my face, anger pouring out from every pore. "Yes, and their momma needs her momma."

Trinia remained quiet for a quick minute before she recovered from the sting in my voice. "I'm sorry. I didn't mean it that way, but who's going to take care of these babies if something happens to you?"

My mind never went down that road before that moment. In my own pain, nothing else mattered at the moment. Trinia allowed me to express my feelings, cry and throw a fit.

After several minutes, she said, "Ok, let's just take one step at a time. Get up, take a shower, and put on some fresh pajamas."

How dare she order me around? But I needed someone like her to gently but firmly guide me. Trinia later shared with me that the night she stayed there, my mother asked her to look out for me. She said it was as if Mom gave her instructions for me. My mother told Trinia she knew God had a calling on my life and to push me no matter what and walk me into my purpose with the help and guidance of God.

I finally got up, took a hot shower and put on fresh clothes.

As I re-entered the room, she asked, "Can you just take the first step for me? That's all I ask."

A fresh wave of anger bore down on me again. Why was she asking me to do something I didn't want to do? "Just let me be. I will decide when I'm ready to do whatever, whenever." How was I supposed to take the first step when I wanted to stay in that same place? And frankly, I didn't care.

Later that night, MaKayla said something to me about Grandma. Then she said it again.

I wondered. Ok, is this a trick?

She just blurted out as if having a conversation with Mother. I didn't know what to make of it.

One day MaKayla said, "Grandma is going to get you for leaving Pawpaw by himself."

"What?"

She just looked at me.

Then while riding in the car, she blurted out, "Look at Grandma in the sky on that cloud!"

I promise I almost ran off of I30 near Oakland Blvd.

Then again on that same freeway, she said, "Look at Grandma on top of that big blue thing." She pointed to a big blue water tower off I30.

I didn't say anything and wondered which of us might really be losing our minds.

A few months went by, and we took a family vacation to Florida.

MaKayla came in the room again, saying something about Grandma.

Ok, this needs to stop.

Then one day, my dad made a statement. "You can't take MaKayla anywhere with you. That girl almost made me wreck the car. She starts talking about Grandma, asking me 'Do you see Grandma, Pawpaw?'"

I believe they had a small incident Daddy failed to tell me about, but MaKayla shared every time we went a certain direction. "Pawpaw's car was over there in the ditch."

Even today, I'm not sure what ditch, but I do know he called AAA at one point and time to get his car out of a ditch. What seems quite comical as I think about it now didn't amuse me then.

In this life, we can experience some ditch encounters. We fall so low in the pit, we can't see our way out. Those times in your life, you need to have at least one true friend you can count on—one who will be honest with you, help pull you out of the pit and not have a pity party with you. It's vital to have one key person who tells you the honest truth, whether you want to hear it or not.

During my school years, while experiencing some major peer pressure and my first heartbreak, I thought the world ended. I walked around with a big knot in my stomach, afraid to see the person who broke my heart. Even worse, what if I saw him with another girl?

"Oh my, I can't handle that," I told myself while getting dressed for school.

A really close friend at the time realized how deeply I agonized over the situation. She got in my face. "Girl, come on. Keep it moving. You are going to be just fine. It's his loss, not yours."

What was she thinking? I blurted out, "You don't understand."

"Let me tell you like my grandma told me," she said. "There's more fish in the sea."

That statement really confused me. What did fish in the sea have to do with my pain? And how did that help when my heart ached for that one boy? But she remained honest with me. She reminded me that I deserved more. She asked the hard question, why I cried over spilled milk. In that moment of pain, I needed someone bold enough to speak those words to me.

A sweet lady full of wisdom once told me, you can't tell your heart who or who not to love. Your heart opens to the attraction of what is spoken through your ear gates, and it's transmitted to your heart.

Do we always choose the right person to fall in love with? Not always. Do we always make the right decisions? No, of course not. What we learn from the choices we made that were not always favorable for us is what counts the most.

The funny thing is, we have a good indication something or someone isn't the best choice, but we are human. We are drawn to feeling needed and most definitely desire love.

I once told my mother when I was in a really bad state of mind, "Why do people describe love as a beautiful thing? To me, sometimes love can be so ugly."

She laughed. "Love has to be sketched into the heart. Love has to be invested into the heart with many deposits. Love don't keep score of mistakes or failures. Love helps pick you up when you have fallen to your lowest point and feel you are at a place of no return. Love never abandons one soul, although it may leave for a season. And if it's meant to be, while patiently waiting, it will return."

Now she messed me up with that. I said, "Mother, love is complicated."

"Oh no, love is not complicated. We make it complicated, trying to force pieces in a place in someone's life that don't fit. You don't force love like you're trying to force an awkward size object in an obsolete space. Love expands and makes room for those hearts that it comes in contact with. Love sustains the vitality of the heartbeat of the relationship."

By this time, I was all in my emotions. Just because I had one bad experience, I was ready to judge everything and every relationship according to that experience. And it became an enemy in my thought process.

What enemy of the mind are you facing? Don't allow your negative thoughts to cause you to miss out on true happiness and or sabotage what's right in front of you. Love is you taking the defining chance, not knowing what's ahead, but trusting God and your heart. You will make positive deposits and get a positive withdrawal.

Again I have a fond memory of a wise woman telling me her best thinking got her in trouble. I laughed every time she told me that. I like having wise women in my life.

She said, "Just when I thought I had it all together, life threw me a curveball, and I reacted without thinking things through before making hasty decisions."

Application Moment:
Key Nuggets shared by my mentor – Trinia James
- *If your mind is not challenged with fruitful things you will always live a mediocre life. Challenge your thinking and build your mind, so you can grow.*
- *"Great minds discuss ideas; Average minds discuss events; Small minds discuss people."*
- *Don't let your present situation dictate your praise. Praise him in spite of—a now praise for a later manifestation.*
- *"Worrying Does Not Empty Tomorrow of Its Trouble, It Empties Today of Its Strength."*

Mrs. Trinia James (my Spiritual Mother & Mentor) passed away in 2010 from complications of sarcoidosis disease. She was a true trooper in my life. She stepped in when I needed her the most because my mother asked her to look out for me and groom me for true ministry. I will forever hold her dear to my heart.

Believers do Battle

When faith is being tested, we often first think, "Oh I'm paying for something I did so wrong in my life."

I learned that's not always the case. You can be the one there every time the church doors open. You can be the one that supports family and friends, gives to the needy, donates your time and money, and believes in honesty and integrity. You may help the stranded person on the side of the road, pay for the person's coffee in front of you in the drive-through line—always a kind Samaritan that offers a lending hand. None of this exempts our faith from being tested. No amount of goodness exempts us from experiencing some type of life trauma or pain.

My mother lived that example before my eyes. She nursed the sick, kept babies, fed the senior citizens in the neighborhood or checked in on them when needed. If anyone deserved to live life to the fullest, it was Mother. If anyone deserved to have heaven here on earth it was my mother. She was always there for everyone who crossed her path.

There's a myth people conceived somewhere along the way and interpreted for others. "Believers don't suffer."

My grandmother shared with me, "This life will bring some type of trouble. Just keep living."

The picture painted for this myth says if you believe in God and have faith, or if you meet some type of status or image, you dodge the bullet of suffering. Let's think about this. Some of the greatest people I know have gone through some type of trial in their lives. For some, it made them stronger and better. For some, the trial made them more appreciative. But for some, it flat out made them bitter and angry, feeling and acting as if the world owed them something.

We all have our own portion and share of this four-letter word called LIFE. I'm reminded of the scripture reading from Job 14:1. *"Man, that is born of a woman is of few days, and full of trouble."* (ESV) I never really made sense of this passage until a few years ago.

Life is full of trouble—for all people. What matters is how we respond to trouble.

How do you define trouble in your life? First, it's uninvited and stays passed its time. Trouble leaves a mess, is never willing to help, and produces expectations far beyond reality. Yes, I talk about trouble like a real person because trouble comes with and through people at times.

I'm laughing very hard as I write this. Why laughing? Glad you asked. I'm laughing because before I matured in the things of life before I got to that place where I stopped allowing people, circumstances and situations to dictate my happiness, I viewed trouble in a different manner.

As I shared earlier, I use to be one that had to be in control. Remember, that came from believing if I was in control, I had control over what I allowed to hurt me. But what happens when things are totally out of your hands? It's like one of those remote-control cars we used to play with as children. The car had to go in the direction the remote directed it. But if the person holding the remote didn't have full control of the remote, sometimes, the handles lost their spring. While operating the remote, the car went its own way. Yet still guided by the remote the car kept moving and often spun out of control and landed in the grass, which brought the car to a complete stop.

That's how trouble operates. It takes advantage of where you are in life and brings life to a complete stop if you allow it. People walk into our lives with baggage. They unpacked their dirty laundry and left it all over the place. There you are trying to clean, wash and fold up their chaos while dealing with your own emotions.

Have you ever had that happen? You were doing just fine, until one day someone just showed up. Oh, you thought this would be a good thing until they started unpacking their emotional baggage in your life. You became their garbage can, and they never took out the trash. You became their dumpster, where they always dumped on you—emotionally, spiritually, financially or physically.

You know that person who borrows your car but never puts gas in it, wears the tires out but never offers to have them rotated or replaced? People come along saying they want to help you but are really a hindrance in your life. And suddenly, you're trying to figure out what and who sent them your direction.

Again, LIFE uses circumstances and situations to train us. My responses in life to certain things are different now. Where I was passive, now I speak up. Where I use to speak too soon, I've learned to be a good listener. And those two things better help me not to mentally battle with myself in certain areas.

Unresolved Issues

During my twelve months of grief counseling, after the death of my daughter, we discovered I had some unresolved pain, wounds and issues. What does that look like? It simply means items in my life were still up in the air, not settled, lingering around, haunting me from time to time. Things I suppressed and refused to face and deal with residing and taking space in my life hindered me from total healing.

Unresolved Grief

We discovered during my counseling that I had not dealt with my mother's death. I kinda swept my emotions under the rug and couldn't face the fact I needed to resolve the unresolved. One of the things that really kept my emotions locked down was the fact I never told my mother exactly what and who violated me as a teenager. It was too hard, and I didn't want her to feel like she failed me.

But that took me over the edge after her death. Thinking back to the summer after her death, I took a girls' trip to a women's conference with several ladies. During the conference, one of the speakers shared that she had not long before lost her mother. She expressed all the things I recently experienced. I cried, I worshipped. I thought I moved forward, but I was still broken on the inside.

As months went on, my grief counselor brought up some common indicators. She bluntly said, "You are still experiencing unresolved grief."

Guess what. I got so mad at her. "Look, lady. I came here for the loss of my daughter. I don't need you hashing up my mother. Let's just get to the point so I can get through this." Honestly, I didn't want to be there in the first place.

She noted, "Well I can't help you with this until we resolve that."

I'm sure anger came out in my tone. "What does this have to do with that?"

She looked at me with compassion. "Everything. Like cooking a hamburger, you don't cook one side of the patty without cooking the other side. The meat will still be undone and raw."

I pondered on that for a minute.

We identified some issues as she asked the following questions:

- *Do you refuse to talk about your loss?*
- *Do you avoid thinking about your loved one who died because good memories are painful?*
- *Do you avoid places or events that remind you of someone who died?*
- *Do you keep the same exact routines you did when they were still alive because you're afraid you will forget*

them?

- *Do you avoid getting close to people? Unresolved grief is usually at the root of fear about any new relationships.*

Is your life forever changed after a loss? Yes. There's nothing wrong with grieving, but you don't have to live the rest of your life in pain.

This part didn't make sense to me when I first heard it. However, as time went on, I often asked myself, what would my mother want for me and my family? Surely she wouldn't want us to spend the rest of our lives living in pain.

But my main question remained. Why did she leave me if she knew this was going to hurt me and the family?

All I kept saying was she would never hurt us. So I spent months trying to figure out what she was thinking and feeling during the moment or moments prior to her death. Were we on her mind? Did she feel we could move on without her?

One of the precious memories came to mind. When my siblings and I gave my dad and her the 40th-anniversary party at a nice hotel, the entire time people asked me why not wait until the 50th. I kept saying, "We want to do this." But something kept nudging in the back of my mind. *Do what you want for your parents. It's not promised that the 50th anniversary will come.* I didn't want any regrets. Therefore, we gave the party, and sure enough, mother passed away right after their 45th wedding anniversary.

Application Moment:

Ask yourself. Is the quality of your life what you want it to be?

Are you locked in time? Are you trapped in a memory that intrudes your mental capacity and peace of mind on a daily basis?

Do you feel guilty for laughing and having a good day?

Do you allow your emotions to spiral out of control followed with depression? Are you opening the mail? Paying bills on time?

Are you experiencing excessive spending habits, shopping or being wasteful?

If you answered any of these questions with "yes," this is a true sign of unresolved grief with moments of depression.

If you answered yes or found yourself in one of these states, please consider some type of grief counseling or finding a local counselor that will walk you through your grief process. Yes, it will take work, but if you do the work you will feel so much better.

Imagine thinking about someone who died, or an ex, without feeling broken hearted. Imagine living and loving to the fullest. What would that be like for you?

Unresolved Trauma

Unresolved trauma can occur from blocked-out trauma during childhood or an emotional event you do not want to deal with in adulthood. However, blocking out trauma does not mean you escape the effects of trauma on your life. No matter how much you deny or dissociate from the trauma, it does not mean the trauma did not happen.

Not dealing with the issues can cause a person to turn to drugs, alcohol, sex, food, shopping, or gambling to push negative feelings away or to numb painful feelings. Realize drugs are not the only addictive substance, although they are the most popular.

Addiction is often an attempt to deal with unresolved trauma or to push it down. If you find yourself using addiction as a way to escape negative feelings, there may be some unresolved trauma to identify with an honest thought process and not falling into the trap of denial, which can lead to other issues. One of these includes eating disorders as a way to attempt to escape from painful feelings. The risk factors for developing an eating disorder include body dissatisfaction, low self-esteem, poor coping skills, and social problems. By controlling your foods and becoming strict on a diet, you may try to escape feelings of sadness or trauma. Regardless of how you escape, disordered eating is harmful to you. I remember not having an appetite after the traumatic experience. That's expected. However, you can't continue to follow in that pattern due to the stress placed on your body. I personally advise seeking therapeutic treatment.

Self-harming often represents an attempt to mask emotional pains too difficult to express. Some people attempt to get relief from emotional pain through physical pain, or self-harm, to distract from life. This behavior leads to self-sabotaging by way of guilt. Self-harming can be a part of unresolved trauma.

Disturbed sleep patterns definitely play a major role. This can lead to self-medicating to fall asleep, which can also lead to a form of addiction. Whether over-the-counter sleep-aids or prescribed medication, dependence on those pills may indicate a deeper issue.

These are some serious areas but necessary to expose and discuss. It is the only way your healing process can begin.

Another important factor to identify is anxiety and panic attacks that may come out of nowhere. Suddenly, you may feel scared of nothing or fearful of everything. Even after the anxiety fades, you may feel unsure why you experienced those symptoms or what brought them on. This is an emotional sign. Something invaded my peace, stole my joy, and fear has become part of who I am. This is where it becomes a must that you get to the root cause of the anxiety. Talk it out and take necessary actions so you won't live in the grip of fear, resulting in a need for anxiety medication.

If you struggle with unresolved trauma, you may

have a deep feeling that you are worthless, bad, or unimportant. You may have low self-worth or internalize negative feelings of yourself. Feeling shame about yourself can indicate a level of unresolved trauma. If you think, "I am bad" or "I am unworthy of love," think about how these beliefs came to be and why you believe them.

Chronic depression is a very serious beast and pitfall of unresolved trauma. If you are depressed, you may feel hopeless, angry or irritable. You might experience self-loathing, a lack of energy, difficulty concentrating, or changes in your eating or sleeping habits. You may feel down, sad, or helpless for no apparent reason. Again, reach out for help.

Your relationships may begin to suffer. You may avoid close friendships or relationships due to a fear of being hurt or rejected, be unfriendly or even hostile to others, have intense but brief romantic relationships, avoid getting "too close" to others, or perhaps even avoid relationships altogether.

On the contrary, you may also seek out relationships with abusive people, take on a victim role, and re-confirm to yourself that you are unworthy of love. Your thinking may become more concrete and childlike. You may cling to incorrect thoughts or beliefs despite evidence that contradicts those beliefs. You may even revert back to thinking patterns you had as a child or create life rules based on your childhood experiences.

For example, if your unresolved trauma involved a male, you may begin to distrust all men or avoid interactions with men thinking they are "bad."

Be aware of Dissociation Syndrome, meaning you feel away from yourself, almost as if you're looking in but not actually in your body. You may space out, become forgetful, lose track of time, create a fantasy world and feel totally detached from yourself. We all do this to some degree, but if you notice yourself feeling this way frequently, pay attention.

Dishonesty is a major issue when dealing with trauma, and sometimes we deceive ourselves most. Don't create lies to cover up your emotions, creating one lie to cover another one. When dealing with any trauma, you may move through difficult feelings rapidly, such as rage, sadness, or generally being upset. Or you may avoid feelings altogether, whether good or bad. You may respond to situations by feeling withdrawn or numb.

All of these signs are serious and could lead to an emotional breakdown. Don't feel ashamed or like a failure if you identified any of the above episodes. Again, immediately seek help.

Can I share that I experienced some of these trauma-related issues? Having a great support team helped me conquer them. I identified a truth I didn't particularly like. I couldn't do it alone and on my own terms. It's not that easy.

Application Moment:

Repeat after me: "As long as this issue is unresolved I cannot move ahead."

Chapter 12
Suffering in Silence

Look closely at how your suffering serves you. Sometimes it is hard to heal because we derive a certain amount of comfort from the pain we know. It is important to ask yourself:

1. *Is my unresolved trauma/hurt/pain an excuse to behave the way I do? (Nobody will blame me—look at what I've been through!)*

2. *Is my pain my identity? (My past, my anger, my depression, my loneliness is all I know how to be.)*

3. *Am I using my hurt, pain and loss to obtain the attention, affection, or love I crave? (He/she loves me because I need them so much.)*

4. *Is my unresolved pain and rejection punishment for someone else? (I want him/her to recognize how they hurt me by my suffering!)*

Finally, as you work through these questions, you may see how they lead to unproductive thinking and behavior. Consequently, you may feel less inclined to live your life plagued by depression, anxiety, self-destructive tendencies, problematic relationships, physical pain, and addiction.

After the death of my daughter, I spent days on the floor of my closet because I didn't want my girls or son-in-law to hear me crying. I was shattered in the closet, laying in a fetal position, aching from inside out, kicking and screaming. But I came out of the closet as if nothing was wrong, pretending to be this strong person full of faith. Until one day, I began detaching from my children. I would leave them with the babysitter, their dad, and even a family friend, too exhausted to pay them any attention. They needed me, but I didn't know how to show them I hurt.

Not only did I lose their sister but their little niece or nephew was gone too. I cried until my face was chapped. The closet was actually my safety net where I could be me. I smiled in front of the church, friends and family because of the label and stigma attached to me from the time we were at the hospital. Doctors fought to save my daughter's life while a big red light flashed above my head. STOP! Here's the lady in all that PAIN. But even then, I wore my badge of faith and strength. No one stopped to notice the lady dying inside from sheer agony.

You can't put a time table on grief. You can't force it to go away. And you can't force it not to exist or even pretend the ripping of your heart never happened. Oh yes, it happened, and I didn't like it. The event causing the grief changed my world and my life.

But remember, it not only changed your world, but it also altered the world around those who live with you and are in your circle and family.

There I was thinking I was the only one hurting. I isolated myself from my other children, although mentally, I reasoned I didn't have the strength to be what they needed as a mother. I learned something about young children—they are stronger than we give them credit for. Today, I can't understand my own actions and why I hid my pain from the children. Was that necessary? No. I believe as a mother it was a form of protection, but I learned sometimes trying to protect others does more harm than good.

My family had already experienced a few hardships prior to the loss of Tori. However, this hardship was really different—more intense. Have you heard the saying, "when it rains it pours?" Not only did events pour down on me, but they flooded my life. One set back hit after the other, pummeling us. I couldn't keep my head above water financially nor emotionally.

Again, I can't understand why I felt a need to protect everyone from the crisis I faced. Maybe it was pride. I didn't want people to know what I was really going through.

I thought I moved past all that. I kept my pain hidden from my father, my siblings, and my entire family. I bravely wore an "oh, I'm good face" while cracking to pieces on the inside.

Back in 2003, I experienced a great deal of hardship. When illness invades your family, it drains your finances and exhausts all your PTO at work.

Immediately after my mother passed away, my daughter, Tori, began to feel sick. She kept having chest pains. We went to the ER where they diagnosed her with a pulled muscle. She continued hurting, so we went to a gastroenterologist (digestive and stomach doctor). He diagnosed her with gallstones. Mind you, she was a very active, healthy senior in high school.

She had surgery to remove her gallbladder. But the pain persisted. What could be wrong?

Several days after her surgery during a follow-up visit, the surgeon said, "Let me take a chest x-ray just to rule out any possibilities of your heart."

This memory is etched in my brain like it happened yesterday. During the Christmas break, with school out and on New Year's Eve, the phone rang. Hearing from the doctor on a holiday surprised me. He called to notify us of Tori's chest x-ray results.

"There is fluid around her heart, and I'm not sure why. Her heart is enlarged. This is very serious."

He immediately called a cardiologist to have her seen, but because of the holiday, offices were closed. The doctor told me if she started feeling worse to take her to the ER. He would be on call, and I was not to hesitate to call his office. The answering service would page him.

And BAMMMM! There come the anxiety and stress intruding in my life again. Still grieving my mother's death, I wondered, "Why is this happening right now?"

I jumped in protective mode. Should I tell Tori the doctor found something wrong?

I didn't have to say anything. She knew already, having shortness of breath and because of the intense chest pains.

Finally, I told her the results and about the need to see a specialist. I watched helplessly as she suffered in her own silence.

"Tori, do you want to talk about it?"

"No, Mom. Not now." I waited for a moment, wanting to be sure. But she shrugged it off and went on with her day.

A few days after the New Year's holiday, the heart specialist saw Tori. At her age, he wondered about the source of her pain. He ran tests and expressed concerns and suspicions about a few things but didn't want to alarm us. Then he gave us options to remove the fluid from her heart. She chose medication. Although she wasn't pleased with all the side effects, she didn't want another surgery.

The specialist ran several blood tests and gave us what he thought might be the problem before test results gave us a conclusive answer.

In preparation for the tests, he asked Tori, "Have

you been under any stress lately? Has anything traumatic happened in your life?"

We looked at each other, questioning. What does that have to do with anything? She was a young 17-year-old, vibrant and athletic. In the marching band at school, awesome volleyball player—what could possibly be wrong?

Then remembering something, I stopped. After a few volleyball games, she told me again that her chest hurt. Then she lost an extreme amount of weight without trying.

We told the doctor, "My mother passed away less than a year ago.

He looked at Tori. "Have you talked about your grandmother's death? Were you close to her?"

She shook her head.

My mother and Tori were extremely close, as I stated earlier. She practically raised both of us at the same time. As a teen mom, many days I had to depend on my mother to take care of her. Just think, my mother was as dear to her as she was to me. She was more Mom than Grandma.

I didn't realize the impact her death had on Tori. She held it deep inside, which greatly impacted her health.

Previously Tori had a cold which turned into a cough. Months before my mother passed away, we went to the doctor. Tori took a few over-the-counter meds. Thinking back, I recalled her blood pressure being high, but the pediatrician figured taking cough medication could have caused that to happen.

We missed the sign of a bigger problem—an underlining issue her pediatrician didn't observe because of other circumstances. Fearing the obvious, the cardiologist voiced suspicions of something seriously wrong—something with her blood or possibly a systemic disease.

After the results came back, we went in a few days later.

The doctor asked a question. "Have you ever heard of Lupus?"

"Lou Who?"

"Lupus or Rheumatoid Arthritis?" He then went on naming all these other "I'TIS."

We looked at each other and shook our heads. "No."

"It appears the blood work shows some form of a systemic disease, but we are not sure what because this is out of my field. I will need to refer you to another specialist—a Rheumatologist."

I looked at him as if he lost his mind. "A RHEU WHO?"

This all sounded foreign, like someone talking to us in another language, and we needed a translator.

Again he looked at Tori and asked, "Have you been traumatized or experienced any type of traumatic stress?"

She finally answered, "Maybe my grandma's unexpected death."

The doctor said, "Grief is as deadly as any disease"

Apparently, Mom's death and the subsequent, suppressed grief caused what slept inside of Tori's body to wake. And once awake, it responded like a tornado, whirling and wreaking havoc in her young system.

The doctor shared with Tori the importance of talking about whatever bothered her, never allowing it to be bottled up on the inside. It wasn't healthy for her.

Again we entered a major crisis. I wanted life to get back to normal, so we moved forward.

The Journey Ahead

From doctor to doctor and appointment to appointment we went. After the first diagnosis, they sent us to another specialist, Dr. Marshall, for confirmation. We didn't like him much. The bed might have shown more compassion. He spoke straight forward, never missing a beat. After visiting with him and confirming the labs, we heard the very words we didn't want to hear.

As we sat in the office, tears streaming down my little girl's face, I kept saying, "It's going to be alright."

She said, "I'm going to school. I've made plans for college, and this is not going to stop me."

"Ok. Let's just take it one day at a time." What else

can a mother tell her baby girl?

Tori finished her junior year, and we went full steam into the summer of her senior year. She had a few challenges and weight gain from the medication. But she stayed on campus at TCU during a summer program. We endured a visit to the ER, and she was back on campus.

She reminded me, "Mom, I'm going off to college."

As she began the medication, fear sat in my soul, mocking me. How can I be miles away from her? What if...?

She was determined. During her senior year, the medication caused weight gain, but she kept pressing through. She continued playing volleyball and leading the Polytechnic High School band as drum major. Determined. This disease would not rob her of life.

After several appointments with the Rheumatologist, they finally identified the type of Lupus that invaded Tori's body—Systemic Lupus.

I researched it more diligently than anything I ever wondered about. Why couldn't it be the one that strictly attacks the skin? However, this diagnosis matched the one that attacks major organs. With Systemic Lupus, the body basically attacks itself. She continued her medication and responded very well. Her heart shrank back to normal, and she prepared to leave for college after graduation.

The strangest thing about life—you can never

predict what lies ahead. There's no forecast to tell you the unexpected is about to happen.

There we were, faced with this devastating news, and I kept thinking only, I need my mother. I needed her beside us, to navigate and advise us on how to process everything at this point in life. Even though the medication helped, it caused severe weight gain and facial swelling. While we prepared for prom, this was very hard. During our mother-daughter time shopping for a dress, depression replaced the joy we anticipated. Nothing looked right. Eventually, Tori decided to have her dress made, and she was happy with her decision.

I tried all I knew to support and be there for her. But I hurt inside as a mother, wanting to fix my baby. And instead of talking it out, I went into isolation again, crying in the bathroom, asking God why. A vibrant, talented young lady with her entire life ahead of her faced a life-threatening disease, and I simply didn't get it. But neither did I dare to share my aching heart with anyone.

One Day at a Time

Life as usual and all we knew existed no more. We continued with scheduled and routine doctor's visits. Graduation quickly approached. I planned a huge dinner party, and we celebrated Tori, showering her with love and support. She continued living life as if nothing was wrong, while I walked around holding my breath, praying this was a mistake. Surely the doctors guessed wrong.

As we began packing her room for college, she had a doctor's appointment. During the visit, we explained that she was leaving for college and attending Sam Houston State University in Huntsville, Texas.

He looked across the room and uttered these shattering words from his lips. "I don't recommend you go away from home."

Big, sorrow-filled tears filled her eyes. She took a deep, steadying breath. "Once again I'm going to school. That's what I've been waiting for since I was in 6th grade—go off to school." She drew in a quivering breath. "At least let me try."

I didn't want to stand in her way because I knew this was important to her. At the same time, fear suffocated me. Yet, I had to trust God and trust her with this one.

My mind and emotions battled, but we packed up and moved her almost four hours away. We made sure all prescriptions were filled until she relocated and could get them from a pharmacy near the campus.

Late October, Tori started not feeling well. The stress of classes and school was a little overwhelming. We later learned stress and Lupus don't get along. She went to the doctor in Huntsville near the campus, but he would not treat her, recommending she visit her family physician at home. After arriving home, she went to the doctor. He advised her again to stay home. Again, she refused. He then told her he couldn't treat her long distance. She drove back to school with her best friend and promised to come home the following week after a test she'd been studying for.

As I sat working a few days later, I got a phone call from the school, telling me she was being rushed to the hospital. I literally went into mental shock, unable to process the news. What? No way. I'm four hours away. Do I drive, fly? How do I get there?

I left Fort Worth with the clothes on my back, leaving my little girls, who were 4 and 6 at the time, with their godmother. I didn't know what to expect.

I kept getting calls with updates. They determined she had a seizure in her sleep, and her friend that was there called 9-1-1. They air-lifted her to Houston Herman Hospital, where we would spend the next week or so.

I prayed so hard on the drive there. "Lord, just let my baby be ok."

Life spun out of control. My heart knotted, my stomach locked, and my sanity completely disappeared. Finally, we arrived, and I made my way to my daughter's bedside. She had several seizures prior to my arrival.

Once the nurse took me to her room, Tori saw my face and her tears flooded.

"I'm here sweet girl. Momma is here."

Later that night, they admitted her to the ICU. I gave them information concerning her medical history. Mind you, the doctor at home wouldn't continue treatment. Every doctor I called had a two-month waiting list. The ER doctor reassured me they would give her the best care. She was in the right place.

They discovered the Lupus caused her blood pressure to escalate, which triggered the seizures. One specialist came in, wanting to aggressively treat her with chemotherapy, but we asked if he would just wait. I spent day and night by her side, realizing I had no change of clothes, toothbrush, money, or hygiene products.

The nursing staff got her settled in and directed me to a local hotel down the street. I went, but my mind stayed at the hospital. Tori was stable by this time, but I couldn't sleep.

The next morning, the doctor met with me to discuss our next steps. He held off on the chemotherapy and tried a different medication. As friends and family around the school and back home prayed for her, we believed God for a miracle.

My greatest support, my sister, joined me. She stayed and supported us during the entire hospital stay. Three days went by and Trinia showed up. The room lit up as she began to pray.

She said, "Tori, I come to take you home." Trinia turned to me. "Go get some sleep. I'll take it from here."

I was so happy to see her—we both were.

The next morning, Tori was doing so well. Her lab work came back and the doctor said, "You don't have to start chemo. We are going to get you home and connected with a good Rheumatologist."

He called ahead and scheduled her without us being on the waiting list. The doctors and nurses kept telling her she was a walking miracle. After having several seizures, it could have been fatal.

We made it home several days later and got an appointment with Dr. Lehman. This time, things began to turn as she responded to the treatment plan. Weak, but she did well.

Now watch this. Can you believe how she went all the way to Houston, the specialist there called back to Fort Worth and got her in to see one of the top specialists here? Now, why couldn't that happen while she was already at home? Again, things happen for a reason. Sometimes it takes going the extended scenic route with a major detour and difficulty to get where you need to be.

Once home and visiting with the new doctor, things proceeded a little bumpy. Tori never wanted anyone feeling sorry for her. Frustrated with the situation, she had plans, and they were on hold.

Many days I spoke the truth. "You know God knew what was ahead. He may have caused a few speed bumps in the road on your path for many reasons we may never know. One thing for sure, life is too precious to be bitter and angry."

This trial did bring us closer together. We had some tough days, disagreements, and arguments. We cried tears, prayed, and fasted. Lord, where do we go from here?

On our drive home, she wanted to stop by her dorm room, see her roommate, and pick up a few things. We had to officially withdraw her from school, which didn't impact her since she enrolled as a second-semester freshman. Later, we returned, packed up her dorm and moved her home.

The entire time, she kept saying, "Momma, I'm coming back to school. "Momma, I'm graduating college."

I reassured her. "You can do whatever you set your mind to do, but you have to be realistic. Sweet Girl, this isn't the end of your dreams."

One night while ambling around the ICU floor of the hospital during the seven-day stay, I walked and talked to God, asking for forgiveness for any and everything I had done in my life.

I desperately pled, "Lord, please let my daughter live and finish college."

As I stood in the hall of the neuroscience floor, I felt a breeze of air hit my neck. Weak in strength, my faith pulled every fiber of who I believed God to be.

In the quietness, a still voice whispered, "Tori will

graduate college. She will get married, and she will be able to conceive a child."

"Lord, I believe."

Driving home, I carried that belief and promise with me.

The doctors took us from one extreme to the next, advising us on what to do, what not to do. Although stressful and mentally exhausting, we held on to each other.

Due to the seizures, Tori wasn't able to drive for six months. Oh my, she was really angry about that.

One day she decided, "I'm going to prove the doctors wrong."

I woke up, and she was gone in the car. Lord my nerves, shattered again, thinking the worse.

In her stubbornness, she determined, "This is not stopping me from living my life."

After several hours, she finally returned home.

I held out my hand. "Give me the keys, please. I know you are hurting, but this is not the answer—to rebel against what we all are trying to do to help you."

"I just want to be normal and live a normal life."

This was a living nightmare for her. A good friend recommended allowing her to vent and release her frustration. At the time, I didn't think she could use a different outlet, and not just me telling her what she could and couldn't do, as the doctors told her.

One day she blurted out, "I'm the one sick. I'm the

one in pain. I'm the one taking 15 pills a day, and this is not fair."

I tried to reason with and encourage her, tried to understand how she felt. I memorized every pill—the name, what it was for, dosage, etc. The most humiliating experience came from applying for disability, going to the hearing and having an occupational therapist tell the judge what type of jobs she could work. The process was so very disheartening.

Tori expressed to the judge how she couldn't sit or stand for long periods of time due to the swelling in her legs and feet. Recovering from a Lupus Crisis, some days she didn't feel up to getting out of the bed.

The judge took notes, asked a couple of questions and told her she would hear from them within sixty days.

As we walked out, she said, "Mom, this was a waste of time, and I had to relive my hospital stay all over again by telling them what I wrote on the paper."

At that moment, I realized people come through the system, wanting disability just so they don't have to work. But there are those who really need it and get denied as she did.

One turning point came when Tori said, "Mom, I'm tired of fighting my fears. I need to open up and talk about this, day-by-day."

We talked more and more, discussing how the sickness made her feel emotionally and mentally. More than a few times, I had to make some tough decisions.

She had only been home a day or two when she called me at work. "Mom?"

"Yes, baby?"

"I think they just cut the lights off. I heard someone on the side of the house. I looked out of the window, and it was the electric company."

With a big lump in my throat, I said, "I'm sorry, baby. It's going to be ok. I was off for two weeks and used all my days, so I didn't get paid. Mom will get the lights back on."

A few days later, the water got shut off, food got low. I robbed Peter to pay Paul. All I knew is I would do whatever it took to keep her happy and safe. Having two small children and my oldest daughter needing me all at the same time was hard.

I was so ashamed to let people know, especially my family, that we needed help. I thought my sister and brothers knew exactly what I needed, and they would just do it. But that wasn't the case.

My sister shared, "I thought you were ok. Every time I asked 'are you good,' you said yes."

I got angry with her and thought to myself, why would you ask me if I'm good, when you know I'm not?

Of course, she believed what I told her. I said I was good, but I really wasn't. I suffered in silence like I always did. And she didn't know how to help me because she didn't know what I needed. My family didn't know my financial situation. There I was working at a big company with benefits. That all looked good, and the company was a wonderful place to work. But remember, I was in the middle of severe hardship, exhausting all of my savings for medication and doctor's visits. I still had bills, daycare, and the cost of living in general. None of that stopped because my daughter got sick. But I kept all of that to myself and kept up the appearance of everything being just fine.

The following spring, the situation turned again. We had several appointments weekly, but soon they became monthly. Tori's vitals stabilized, and she was stronger than ever. She kept pressuring the doctor to release her to go back to school, and finally, he did. So excited, she even enrolled in summer school. After getting a second opinion from a neurologist, she was then released to drive again. Medications were adjusted again, some decreased, and things were getting better. Soon she was in remission.

Application Moment:

Remember you don't have to suffer in silence, you don't have to walk through your crisis alone. Family and friends can't help you if they are not aware of what is going on. It's not a matter of telling all your business, it's just a matter of saying, "Hey, I'm not ok. This is bigger than me, and before it gets the best of me, I need help, whether it's financially, emotionally, or all the above. SCREAM with ME, HELP!

Repeat after me, "I will not allow pride, shame, guilt, or fear to keep me from reaching out for help."

My mother had a saying, a closed mouth won't get fed. As long as you keep your mouth closed and don't tell anyone or ask for what you are in need of, how will you ever know someone can be sent as your guardian angel and blessing. You never know what resources someone can connect you with if you don't ask. Asking for help doesn't make you less of a man or a woman. What you are going through at that very moment is only temporary. Trouble doesn't last always.

"Life is full of unexpected surprises, but if you allow God to be in control, He knows how to make your life come together. Prov. 16:33 says nothing happens by accident. God is in control of everything. So the next time you feel overwhelmed, remember God already got the situation under control." ~Trinia James.

How Do I Get from Here to There

Recently I had a discussion with my 28-year-old niece, Brittany. More like I interviewed her. I remember when my older sister told me she was pregnant.

I laughed so hard. "Girl, you wait until you get 40 to have a baby?"

If you know my sister, she's the more witty and comical one of the family. I call her a goofball, and she doesn't mind me saying so. She's my daily entertainment.

Back to Brittany.

When my sister announced she was pregnant, after she stopped crying, she asked what she was going to do with a baby. Mind you, my sister was never the baby type growing up. She was always so serious. Being around and helped raised by our great-grandmother, she was just different—but a good different shall I say.

I was very excited that she was pregnant and already decided the baby would be a girl. I started thinking of names like this was my baby. The funny part was my oldest daughter, Tori, always stayed with my sister and mother while I worked the night shift. My sister would constantly call me saying your child is hanging off the tree. Your child just fell off the bike. Your child just jumped the fence, and she's getting on my nerves.

So, she's pregnant with Brittany, and Tori was in the first grade.

When she called one night I told her, "You are the babysitter. Take control. You will have your own child soon."

Tori and LaJoyce would be in constant battles.

I kept telling my sister, "She's preparing you for motherhood. It will be funny if your baby is born on Tori's birthday. Well, guess what? Long story short, Brittany was born January 24, 1991, on Tori's birthday. It was hilarious to me. I laughed so hard.

To say the least, Tori was upset this baby was coming, taking the light off of her, and my sister was like oh my goodness.

I smiled and said, "I told you."

As time went on, Tori and Brittany bonded and were close like sisters although technically cousins.

During my sister's pregnancy, the doctors discovered she had the sickle trait. Although my mother knew about it, nothing was ever discussed concerning her having children. The doctors gave my sister a 90% chance Brittany would be born with sickle cell.

After visiting a couple of specialists, the doctors advised her to abort Brittany at that time. The devastation of hearing those words was so heartbreaking, my sister went into a deep depression. Mentally, she lost all focus.

My mother prayed and told her, "We will trust God. He doesn't just give life, He gives it with a purpose."

"Well, it's settled," My sister told the doctors. "I will not abort." And she carried on with the pregnancy.

Once Brittany came, they ran many tests, confirming she had sickle cell anemia. She faced a few challenges as a baby, in and out of the hospital. I still have a vision of her when she was around 7 months old. Admitted into the hospital for a sickle cell crisis, she stood up in the hospital crib, all bright and bubbly with her big eyes beaming at me.

I kept looking at her. "You don't act like you are

sick."

She kept right on bouncing up and down. Then she whimpered a little because she couldn't tell us if she hurt or didn't feel good. But that look she gave me is still embedded in my memory—a look of strength, the look of a fighter in the boxing ring.

From that day she had many good days and bad, but I always saw the fight in her eyes.

Today, Brittany is one of my inspirations. She's vibrant and strong. During my recent conversation with her, I asked if I could insert a mini-interview in this book. She eagerly agreed.

I've watched through the years as she faces many challenges. Things we take for granted daily, Brittany never experienced as an adult. As I began to ask questions during our discussion, one was how she perseveres when faced with physical challenges? How do you not let your mental state sabotage your physical push?

Brittany shared with me, she perseveres each day by pressing through her physical condition and mentally focusing on and remembering her promises from God. Not dwelling on her limitations or inabilities, she lives with an expectation of seeing life through the lenses of Christ one day at a time.

She said, "Auntie, I know trouble don't last always. I can't focus on what I can't fix. I fix my faith in who I know has the purpose of my life in His hands."

Brittany's focal point is spiritually trusting God and knowing she's a walking miracle.

"Mentally, I can't afford to let my thoughts consume me or take me to a place of no return. I don't focus on the pain or disappointment. I have to solely focus on looking forward to the next second, minute and day that life has for me."

At a tender age, she was forced to start renal dialysis. This limits her ability to travel, swim, or go into big crowds. But oh let me tell you—she's on the praise team at church, sings and dances as if there's no tomorrow. She realizes she hasn't accomplished all she desires in her life, due to a physical condition, but she's blessed to still be here. She desires a normal life like you and I. This is where she has to stay inspired through the Word of God and music.

When she sees others taking life for granted, that triggers her biggest battle. She questions why people don't understand what they have. Why do they abuse their bodies and their relationships with loved ones? Or even why they are just flat out mean as a junkyard Pitbull.

If they only knew, life is but a vapor. *"Yet you do not know [the least thing] about what may happen in your life tomorrow. [What is secure in your life?] You are merely a vapor [like a puff of smoke or a wisp of steam from a cooking pot] that is visible for a little while and then vanishes [into thin air]."* (James 4:14 AMP)

We must appreciate every second of life we are afforded here on earth.

Brittany understands the frustrations many people have, young and old, who are limited due to certain medical conditions. With anything, you want to have a normal day and a normal world. But when you have limited mobility or limitations to the things you desire to do, such as travel, have children, work a full-time job, etc., you can find yourself being angry as she did at one point in her life. Honestly, she still does at times. But she identified her anger and manages her emotions toward the situation without allowing it to take her over the edge. As well as being angry with God by having a moment, she thinks through it without overthinking. Then she talks it out with her husband and gains spiritual guidance from her Pastor (which happens to be her Auntie, aka "ME").

She stated that after talking with her husband, and if it upsets him that she's having a rough day because he can't fix it, they immediately pray together. Their daily devotion to God and each other allows them to lean on one another, each encouraging the other through prayer and faith in believing God has a purpose and plan.

Brittany remembers her focal point stating, "We walk by faith and not by sight, leaning on the everlasting arm of God."

I asked Brittany what were some things she would

like to share with readers who have a physical disability, sickness or are experiencing hardships.

"Some people are anointed to suffer. Sometimes they should ask God, 'How are you getting the glory out of this? Why would you allow sick people to be born into the earth who can't take care of themselves, who feel like they are a burden on their caregivers?' How does this glorify Him?"

Her greatest testimony came during one of her crises, which included a week-long hospital stay. She asked questions we all ask.

Lord where are you? What do you do when you know you TRUST HIM, but YOU can't TRACE HIM! Lord, did you forget about me?

Instantly, she states, "Auntie, we all have a cross to bear. Yours just might not be as heavy as mine, and mine may not be as heavy as yours (moment of tears)."

Her encouragement to those experiencing some type of physical disability is to NEVER GIVE UP! I know that sounds easier said than done. The key is you can't go by what it looks like. Yes, you keep getting news from the doctors. Ok, but my faith is elevated in believing God who created me is the same God who will deliver me. When you have nothing else but Him, that's all you have to hold on to. I heard a song that reminded me of Brittany, the words captured my heart—"You're built to last."

Mrs. Brittany Shemil is blessed and a very happy

and outspoken young lady who loves the Lord. She has a wonderful husband who treats her like a queen. I commend them both for the road that has been tailor made to journey. Thank You, Lord, that my sister didn't listen to the doctors and abort this beautiful soul, not that I thought she would. Brittany has brought such joy into my life and the lives of others.

Thank you, Brittany, for being my inspiration and allowing me the opportunity to interview you.

Application Moment:

When we are faced with certain battles or crises in life, we tend to isolate ourselves as we wrestle with being in denial—hey look. Something is wrong, and I can't do anything to fix it. Here are a few key factors we should apply and process through during these moments:

1   *Acknowledge there is an issue.*
2   *Accept the positive and fruitful help that others offer.*
3   *Don't beat yourself up.*
4   *Face the issue head on—the longer you sit in denial, the harder it is to make progress.*
5   *Don't waste precious time fighting fear. Take a leap of faith and trust that everything is working together for your good.*

Chapter 13
Failure is not Fatal

Failure. Defeat. Destruction. Despair. These are just some of the words we think about when our lives come crashing down in front of our eyes. Failure can be catastrophic. It can wreak havoc and take us on a mental and emotional trip we would much rather not go on. But failure has a purpose. There's a reason we fail in life. When we're in the midst of the pain, we oftentimes can't see that reason. We can't witness the bigger picture when we can only see the hurt in front of our eyes.

<u>Understand that Failure Isn't the End... It's a New Beginning</u>

Depending upon how you look at your situation and all that's surrounding it, you should come to realize failure isn't the end.

When Walt Disney was fired from his job at the Kansas City Star in 1919, the editor of the paper said he "lacked imagination and had no good ideas." But that wasn't his last failure. Walt Disney went on to purchase an animation studio named Laugh-O-Gram, which he later drove into bankruptcy. Failure most certainly wasn't the end for Walt Disney, as we very well know today.

Life's "mountains" can be hard, even for the best of us. A "mountain" can make you want to "go around it," when in actuality, the best way to conqueror it is to either go "through it" or get "over it." If we go through it or over it, we gain experience for the next mountain that comes as opposed to going "around it" and finding out the next one is the same size and we have no idea how to handle it either.

Yep, it's a struggle. But how we go "through it" determines how we "look" when we come out on the other side. I might look like I've been through it, but as long as I'm still standing in the ring when the bell sounds, I WON! Welcome to "Through-The-Struggle" Quote by Pastor Michelle Jones.

Application Moment:

This is a good time to pause, here the application moment is earlier than in previous chapters. Why is that? Now it's time to reset and recalibrate your thinking and mindset.

When change is interjected into our lives, it may not come in the order you think it should. So our thinking has to be reset, broadened, as we view life with an open mind. Things don't always look the way they seem.

Repeat after me. "Today I recalibrate the settings of my

thinking process. This is how my healing begins."

Tell yourself, "It's my season because God said it's time." Daniel 2:21 reminds us He is the God that changes seasons and times. He turns kings' hearts anyway He wants to. So rest in Him and allow God to do what He started. The greater Greater in your life.

Recently I took a medical coding class. It was more complex than I thought. However, I enjoyed learning how the doctor's office and hospitals process the billing of medical treatment, and I gained some insight into how the insurance companies decide whether to pay. When the claim is received by the insurance company, it's all in how the bill of services is coded and processed. Funny, one code off or if the insurance company needs additional information and it's not received, the claim can be rejected. The patient will end up with an unnecessary bill, although they have insurance coverage. The claim must be processed according to standards of the company in order to be paid.

So listen, our healing plays a role, such as a rejected claim. There were times when I thought my healing process was part of someone else's responsibility if they claimed they loved and cared about me. As men and women, we've all been in relationships that have gone or grown sour, in friendships that became fatal, experienced family issues that had you torn between two worlds. You know that love-hate relationship. I love them but hate what they did to me.

So as I took this class, something stuck in mind about how claims are presented. For example, with a wound or burn wound, you can't just be seen or treated by the physician one time and never go back to have it checked. Wounds have a process, a time of healing. Wounds have stages during the process. Let me describe this for you more in detail using medical terminology.

When the skin is injured, our body sets in motion an automatic series of events, often referred to as **"the cascade of healing"** in order to repair injured tissue. **The cascade of healing is divided into these four overlapping phases: Hemostasis, Inflammatory, Proliferative, and Maturation.**

- **Phase 1: Hemostasis Phase** - the first phase of healing begins at the onset of injury, and the objective is to stop the bleeding. In this phase, the body activates its emergency repair system, the blood clotting system, and forms a dam to block the drainage. During this process, platelets come into contact with collagen, resulting in activation and aggregation. An enzyme called thrombin is at the center, and it initiates the formation of a fibrin mesh, which strengthens the platelet and clumps into a stable clot.
- **Phase 2: Defensive/Inflammatory Phase** - the

second phase, called the Defensive/Inflammatory Phase, focuses on destroying bacteria and removing debris — essentially preparing the wound bed for the growth of new tissue.

- **Phase 3: Proliferative Phase** - Once the wound is cleaned out, the wound enters Phase 3, the Proliferative Phase, where the focus is to fill and cover the wound. The Proliferative phase features three distinct stages: 1) filling the wound; 2) contraction of the wound margins; and 3) covering the wound (epithelialization).

During the first stage, shiny, deep red granulation tissue fills the wound bed with connective tissue, and new blood vessels are formed. During contraction, the wound margins contract and pull toward the center of the wound. In the third stage, epithelial cells arise from the wound bed or margins and begin to migrate across the wound bed in leapfrog fashion until the wound is covered with epithelium. The Proliferative phase often lasts anywhere from four to 24 days.

- **Phase 4: Maturation Phase** - During the Maturation phase, the new tissue slowly gains strength and flexibility. Here, collagen fibers reorganize, the tissue remodels and matures and there is an overall increase in tensile strength (though maximum strength is limited to 80% of the pre-injured strength). The Maturation phase varies greatly from wound to wound, often lasting anywhere from 21 days to two years.

The healing process is remarkable and complex, and it is also susceptible to interruption due to local and systemic factors, including moisture, infection, and maceration (local); and age, nutritional status, body type (systemic). When the right healing environment is established, the body works in wondrous ways to heal and replace devitalized tissue.

We just saw the process of how a wound to our physical body must go through a process. The one part I really focused in on was Phase 3 – the wound has to be cleaned out from all debris. If not, this can make the wound infected, slow down the healing process or affect other parts of the physical body.

The same is true with our emotional wounds, broken heart, wounded souls. The debris must be cleaned out. Forgiveness and letting go must take place.

"The pain has to be revealed in order for the hurt (wound) to be healed."

You must keep telling yourself, "This pain is not the end of my story." This is not a life sentence that keeps you locked as a prisoner inside of your pain.

Rejection plays a vital role in our healing process. REJECTION—substandard, inadequate, devalued, scorned, humiliated, unwanted, a failure, not good enough. Do you feel crushed by the experiences of life and can't believe you'll ever be able to make the grade? Never feel good enough? Were you compared with siblings and/or others who had abilities different from yours? Were you abandoned by a parent or in a relationship? Did someone in authority—police, CPS, counselor, pastor, youth leader, coach, teacher—completely abandon you after they promised to help and you confided in them?

Often, these past experiences of rejection sow into our beliefs about who deserves to be accepted and loved. These beliefs lead us to judge others, who in turn judge us and often reinforce our beliefs about our own unacceptability.

Perhaps the most damaging result of these experiences is that they may lead us to assume God assesses our worth in the same way. But that is absolutely wrong!

When a sense of worthlessness crowds in, feelings of rejection overwhelm us. Childhood sexual abuse typically results in a sense of rejection—not only by others who were intended to protect and nurture us and from our perpetrator(s), but also from ourselves as we feel totally unacceptable.

In truth, UNCONDITIONAL ACCEPTANCE and a SENSE of BELONGING is our inheritance through Jesus Christ. NOTHING we do, even our disobedience, can or will stop God from loving and accepting us. His love is not conditional upon our behavior, as His mercy and grace are the same for everyone.

He unconditionally ACCEPTS everyone.

We don't earn it, and we don't deserve it—it is just

there!

I want you to understand, your failures are not fatal to the point that this is the end of your life. Ok, you failed a class, your marriage failed, you job failed, your finances failed. There's a new chapter being written for your life.

I ministered the message "The Teacher & the Test." The teacher who gave the lessons stands next to us during our greatest test, one we really didn't study for. Somehow we thought we had the answers. Funny how during a test, the classroom gets real quiet. As you read the test, you see the questions and some appear as trick questions.

What about when you studied the lessons the teacher gave you throughout the course of the class (life) and you still feel like you failed? God knows what He put in each of us. During times when He doesn't speak, those are times He waits on you to believe in yourself—that you can pass the test in front of you.

Life experiences train the heart and mind to believe I can triumph over tragedy and disappointment. Or shall I just sit here and die? The training of the heart and mind gives you wisdom and understanding. Strong people aren't born—they are made in the heat of the flames of a fiery furnace. They are made in the heat of the test "Built to Accomplish and Survive."

Do you not know you can survive from the shattered pieces of life?

How? First by choosing to get up and live after a shattering life-altering experience hits your life.

Buried hurts stay alive and fester, causing us to continue to be shaped and motivated by the unrecognized pain and associated inner beliefs about our unacceptability. TRUTH and REALITY about our behavior is a necessary starting point for our healing.

Take note—self-deception is a very slippery path. A rebellious person starts by becoming their OWN authority in behavior and lifestyle, and by so doing, they cut themselves off from all accountability to any higher authority. They become their own higher authority. In essence, they become their own god! I'm reminded in one passage of scripture, Paul warns if we stray from desiring the lordship of Jesus and His truth, then eventually, delusion will follow and bring destruction.

The Healing Process Hurts

May 2010, I fell and shattered my ankle, literally breaking it in many pieces.

I was away from home in Des Moines, Iowa for a ministry assignment and went to breakfast. Upon returning to the hotel, I looked away, actually being nosey, didn't see the curb and slipped and fell. Lying there on the ground, I knew it was bad.

My leg immediately went numb and both my feet were curled under me. I just kept looking up, saying,

"Stay focused. You are on assignment."

Fortunately, a retired nurse saw me fall from a distance and immediately rushed to me. As the hotel manager tried to lift me up and put me in the van, the nurse screamed, "Don't move her. Call 9-1-1."

My dear friends accompanying me on the trip were just as shocked as I was. This occurred right before the time for me to be at the program to speak. I remained calm and told them it was going to be ok. But I knew it was bad.

The hospital was across the street, but I couldn't get up and walk, both legs injured.

One young lady with me looked down and asked, "Did you fall?"

I thought to myself, "Well maybe I didn't. Maybe I'm dreaming. Why would she ask me if I fell, seeing me laying on the ground in this gravel?"

The nurse who came over to help me said, "Stay calm."

Instead, I heard her ask if I hurt anywhere else. I said, "I don't think so."

She did a preliminary evaluation and stated the worst possibilities, and then said, "Let's get you across the street."

The paramedics, fire truck and ambulance, made it within five minutes. They talked me through the process of getting me off the ground and on the stretcher. Because they weren't sure of any other injuries, they put my neck in a brace.

I protested. "I don't think I need this."

"It's for precautionary reasons," they reassured me.

So strange how one break in a single area can damage connected areas. I appreciated the kind and gentle transport from the ground to the stretcher by those attending to me. Everyone stood around, encouraging me. But I was ashamed. How did this grown lady fall? How ridiculous. Everything in my brain flashed before me. My children didn't like for me to travel without them.

Jaslin specifically told me, "Don't get hurt and be safe."

How was I going to explain this to my girls who already went through so much? Here was yet another shattering moment in their little lives.

Finally, they wheeled me into the ER. Memorial Day weekend, late Saturday afternoon, and to my surprise, an orthopedic surgeon was on call, tending the ER. Everyone cheerfully entered the room upon my arrival and asked all type of questions.

I responded, "I'm from Fort Worth, Texas. I was being nosey, wondering why all these military people are on the bus in front of my hotel. Where are they going, and what are they doing? I looked down at my phone, and boom, I'm on the ground."

I looked at the doctor. "Now listen. You have two hours to patch me up, so I can get to my ministry assignment." I smiled. "Please."

The doctor shook his head. "Let's wait a minute. First, we need to run some tests, get x-rays and see how severe the break is. We need to clean the wound."

I had a break in the skin (see there's that word again—debris). I translated it as trash and dirt in the wound.

He continued, "Let's get it all clean up. We must assess the wound to assure the bone didn't break through the skin. The doctor and nurse gave me the worst case scenario. "If the bone is through the skin, you will be staying with us for a few days."

"No sir, I have somewhere to be, and I've got to get back home after this assignment."

I started praying, talking to my feet and commanding my bones to be healed. They couldn't give me anything for pain until they decided if I needed immediate surgery.

I bargained with them. "If y'all patch me up, give me a wheelchair, let me go to the program, then I will come back immediately after it is over."

Everyone in that room laughed at me. I didn't see the humor in any of it.

Immediately, the x-rays came back. The bone didn't break the skin, but the break of my ankle was ugly. The x-rays were literally foggy and dark. What a mess.

So the doctor told me, "Ok, here's the plan. The wound is clean with no bone fragments in it. (Good news.) We cleaned it, and the next step is to put you under and set your leg back into place." He grew solemn. "Take us seriously. You have 72 hours to have surgery. We can do it here, or you can fly back home."

I told them, "I will fly home immediately when I'm finished."

I prayed. They talked, then put me under, giving me what they called a "Michael Jackson" cocktail.

"What in the world? No, Michael is deceased."

They laughed. "No, it's the medication he was taking. You won't feel or remember anything. You'll be out for like 15 minutes."

"Ok, let's do this."

Focused on why I was there, I didn't panic. I prayed as the nurse put the medication in my IV. I began to talk about Tori, and I don't remember anything after that.

My dear friends who were with me and scared senseless later told me the nurses and doctors grew emotional, tearing up because I shared with them about my daughter passing away a year earlier.

They said, "You are very strong, and we are sorry this happened to you."

Fast forward, they released me from the ER with a wheelchair and crutches, and I made it to the church.

Everyone was shocked. "What happened to you? We just saw you at breakfast."

I finished my assignment that Saturday night and Sunday morning. Monday I headed on my way back to

DFW. The flight was hard, but I made it.

Once I arrived home, I thought, "Well, it's the holiday. I can wait until Tuesday."

That didn't happen. I hurt too badly. I actually went to the ER after arriving at the airport, but then told my sister, "Just take me home. I can wait until tomorrow."

But I started not feeling well and decided to return to the ER. Thank goodness I did. When I got there and they removed the temporary cast and bandages, my leg was holding moisture, which was dangerous and almost at the point of getting an infection.

They took more X-rays, admitted me into the hospital and called for the orthopedic surgeon on call. Once I was seen by the surgeon, he prepped me for surgery the next morning. Oh did I have a rough night? Fear set in and rode me hard.

"Lord, will I lose my leg? Don't let me get an infection."

I started running a fever in the middle of the night, and they started giving me antibiotics. My blood pressure went up, then down. I worried about my girls who needed me. They were extremely upset when they found out I had to stay in the hospital. I went into panic mode, not knowing what to expect.

The next day, the nurse on the morning shift came into the room, taking really good care of me. I finally told her I was having anxiety because I was worried about the surgery and my leg.

I allowed fear and doubt to settle in after being the strong one in Iowa. "I was strong and fearless in Iowa. How did I get home and become afraid?"

The nurse was so sweet. She kept talking to me and then said, "Let me show you something." She pulled up the pants leg of her nice blue scrubs and showed me a huge scar. "I was walking in some ten-inch high heels on my way to a function. While walking across the grass of the walkway, my foot went in a sinkhole. I didn't see it, but I heard my leg snap, and immediately I was on the ground." She put her pants leg back down. "Your break is not as bad as mine was. I had to be care-lifted to the hospital."

She nursed me with grace because she experienced a similar break and extended compassion. As she wrapped my leg, she assisted in giving me what was called a **Betadine Liquid Bath**. Betadine rapidly kills bacteria, fungi and viruses commonly responsible for wound and skin infection. You remember reading as I shared about cleaning out the wound, so the process of healing can start.

"Listen," the nurse said. "I want to soothe your fears. You are going to survive the break." She washed me with the solution, scrubbed my arms and upper legs. "There will be no contamination during surgery that will cause an infection in the break of the skin."

Let me pause here. Sometimes, things can break us down and bring us to our knees in life, and the other parts of us are infected by the break. It damages and contaminates due to the infection inside us from the wound left in our hearts and the mental state the break afflicted.

But catch this. She said, "During your surgery, we don't want the abrasions of the skin to be compromised by any foreign particles."

I still remember those words. How many times do we allow things to compromise who we are? To circumnavigate who we've been tailored made to be? Built with a purpose, for a purpose, and on purpose by the hand of life, others or even God, we experience a break that causes our lives to be altered forever.

The surgery lasted a few hours—long and intense. But it was a success.

After pins, plates, and screws (the hardware) were put in place to reconstruct my ankle, I thought, "Ok this is cool. I will be up and around, back to normal in no time."

Think NOT!

The surgeon came in the next morning, and boy I was in pain. The recovery hurt worse than the break itself. "When I fell, my foot was dangling off, but Lord, it feels like something is burning the inside of my leg in this cast."

After I did my complaining, the doctor continued to explain that my recovery would be long and hard. He prescribed home health, as well as a nurse to visit weekly, and both occupational and physical therapy. He instructed me NOT to put any pressure on my foot until after he saw me in the office in 10 days to remove the staples.

After four days in the hospital, I finally made it home. I had to sleep in a recliner and sit on an adult portable potty-chair like a toddler. A medical supply company delivered a wheelchair, walker, shower chair, and other items I needed for rehabilitation.

When he came in, I looked at that man. "Sir, where are you going with all this stuff? I'm fine. I won't need this."

He might have turned his back so I couldn't see him snickering as he brought it all inside.

Well, I guess you can imagine, my assessment wasn't true. By the third day at home, I cried for a shower I couldn't' take. Totally helpless, I couldn't take care of myself. For some odd reason, I felt much weaker than before the surgery.

When reality hit, it pummeled me. "Girl, you can't take care of yourself. You can't even get a drink of water." Besides the physical pain, my mental capacity totally checked out too. Not good. Life again spinning out of my control.

The office visit to have the cast and staples removed brought with it the most mind-boggling experience words can't even express. Pain so intense, I took pills prior to going, but that didn't help. To top it off, the most humiliating part of the visit was when I had to go over to the next room to get an x-ray.

The male nurse working there was so insensitive. "Get up on the table."

"Uhhhh, sir, my leg is hanging off."

He looked at me with a "your problem" look. I had to grab my leg, hold it up and put it on the table. My leg moved, out of control due to lost muscle tone. I made it back to the exam room, where the doctor insisted I try wearing a boot after getting the staples out.

Now you can only imagine the scene. He forced this big, fat, swollen ankle into a big, black boot, and I knew that wasn't going to work. I will never forget as long as I'm alive. This all happened on Friday.

By the time I got home, the office was closed. "Nope, not working. I'm in too much pain."

The home health nurse visited me the next day. I couldn't handle the pain. All weekend I was in distress and tears. Finally, Monday came with me back in the office, begging for another cast to be put on my foot.

To my surprise, the surgeon agreed. He told me he had to bend my foot because of the hardware to make sure it set appropriately. If not, I would have a limp for the rest of my life. I only knew my ankle needed some support the boot just couldn't give, and the pain was too great. He put the cast on, and I felt better. Yet, the pain remained intense.

Soon the physical therapist started her visits three

times a week. She was aggressive.

I asked, "Can you please take it easy?"

"It's important that you not lose muscle mass while lying in the bed, not able to be mobile."

One day she was more aggressive than others, the two of us getting in it all afternoon. She kept trying to get me to do more, and I said, "No, that's too painful."

Not realizing she reported this all back to the doctor, I couldn't wait to tell him how mean she was at the next visit. I itched to tell him she's taking me too fast, and it's too painful to do what she asks of me.

After my exam, I started in on how I didn't like my physical therapist. He asked me why, and I kept going on and on, ending with my summation. "It hurts, and she's rough."

The doctor responded, "Well if you told me you liked your physical therapist, and she was wonderful, then that would have let me know she's not doing her job."

What? I wanted sympathy and a new therapist, not what he said.

He continued. "Helena, rehabilitation is not going to feel good. But what's required of you to help you regain your mobility is good for you. The pain has a purpose in your rehab. You have to allow it to produce the mobility you lost and the strength you shall gain."

If I tell you the truth, I sat there mad at him—and her. I thought my recovery was going to be easy. After the break, I could shower, get to the restroom without assistance. But after the surgery, after the fix, after the repair, then came the rehabilitation to restore what was lost. That produced far more pain than the break.

Are you catching what I'm saying? The recovery, restoration, regrouping hurts greater than the initial break.

The process of healing hurts, and it's not as easy as it looks. We find ourselves asking the question, "Was it the break that was the problem or is it the pain of the recovery?"

Well I come to tell you—through my recovery, I discovered recovery can sometimes be ugly and painful, but it's necessary.

After he put the second cast on, I had to wear it throughout the summer—the hot Texas summer. And I was miserable, pretty much stuck in the house all day. Finally, I got the cast off and another boot put on. The second time wasn't as bad. It still ached, but I tolerated it much better. Ready for the next level of physical therapy, so I thought.

Instead of her coming to me, the time came to go to the physical therapy facility. This level of rehabilitation taught me how to care for my scar. Oh my. I didn't know this was going to be that disgusting. As my skin healed, the dead skin shed. The old fell off, and the new skin formed, but let me tell you something, I thought I was scarred for life. So ugly, my foot was dark, bruised and swollen.

During this process of my rehabilitation, one therapist worked on the inside of my ankle, the muscles. She did this technique where she massaged the scar of my stitches and staples, telling me that was to break up the scar tissue. When I say painful, oh my Lord. Painful doesn't even come close to the description.

So there I was having to learn how to walk all over again. She taught me how to use my walker once I was able to put pressure on my foot. The other therapist taught me how to manage the care of my skin and scar. She told me what oils to use, when and how to soak my foot. Then I had to get those lovely, stylish (NOT) compression socks to keep the swelling down. All a process.

While recovering, I ordered some three-inch heeled boots from the QVC shopping channel. Those boots arrived, motivating me to stay the course of rehabilitation and physical therapy. I wanted to look cute in those boots. And yes, it took over a year before I could wear them.

I shared my physical break with you to give some insight into how things can impact our lives that we must and will be restored from. However, the rehabilitation process can sometimes, be painful and ugly. We must start on the inside with the root cause of the initial break. Don't allow pain to eliminate the process of healing. I made a full recovery, and my ankle is doing well.

You Are Not Alone

A few years later, as I was on my way to a doctor's appointment, something unexpected happened! I fell again—down the stairs in the parking garage. How did that happen? I don't know. One minute I was walking and talking to my husband who was walking beside me, and suddenly I was flat on my stomach and knees! I had a flashback of my previous fall in 2010.

But that's how LIFE can be—an unexpected blow or fall. As I sat there with my eyes closed, I could hear his voice, but I couldn't respond.

He kept saying, "Are you ok? Baby get up."

My purse lay underneath me, but somehow I was yet holding on to the strap!

A lady ran over to us. "Are you ok? Let me help."

But my husband responded, "I got her!" He gently touched my arm. "When you are ready, stand up and just lean on me. I got you!"

As he helped me up, I leaned all my weight on him, and he began to examine me.

He said, "Open your eyes."

One lady said, "I will get you a wheelchair."

But I refused the wheelchair. Keep in mind, my doctor's office was only a few feet in front of me, just where I took the fall. Almost at my destination, but I fell.

Today I want you to know, you can get up and just lean on Jesus. He's walking right beside you, and remember the most important thing. He already knew when you fell down, you would need Him to help you get back up!

I wasn't hurt seriously, and I definitely got a revelation out of my unexpected fall. Get up and LEAN (trust God)!

The thing that broke you down to your knees is the very thing God is using to elevate you. Tell yourself, "I'm on my way UP from here." It was necessary for my making of elevation.

Moment of Encouragement

What's broken can be mended. What's hurt can be healed. No matter how dark the issues of life may seem, remember the sun is going to rise again and you are too.

With a heart of gratitude and mind filled with thankfulness, as I look back over my life, God has been so good to me. There was a time I gave up on everything and everyone in life because I was angry. I even took a sabbatical from ministering.

My testimony is simple. He's the God who heals broken hearts. I never thought my life would be filled with such joy after such tragedy and loss, never thought I would smile from the inside out. And I really don't know when I stopped being angry with God for allowing such pain.

One day I had a talk with Him. I came at him point blank, blunt and holding nothing back.

"Lord, I'm mad at you, and this is more than I can handle. You allowed this to be. I realize I can't live like this or tolerate this hurt that's so deep in my soul. I refuse to minister in this condition."

One day my girls came to me.

"We need to talk," Jaslin said to me. "Why are you quitting now? You better go back and preach and let the rest of life take care of itself."

MaKayla joined in. "Yeah, Mom. It's weird not hearing you pray. That's all we know. I think you better get busy. We got you."

Now, these are the same two who use to tell me that I prayed too long. I had to laugh at the thought of them telling me to pray again. God used them to bring joy and healing to my life.

Just want to share, you never know who might encourage you along the way. This is what being Healed 4 Real feels like when your peace is greater than your problem.

Sitting here, I thank God for deliverance. Today I really feel free.

I was thinking back about a time not many years ago when I was so angry with God and mad at the world because of all the pain and disappointment that left me utterly broken. Preaching and mad at the same time. Going to church bitter. I look back and laugh at the irony of that time in my life.

One day I said, "Let me go sit myself down somewhere until I can get some help. And if God who says that He loves me, my creator who has allowed all this turmoil, until He does something with me, I'm nothing until I can help myself."

Many days I asked questions and never got an answer, until one day I was ready to hear "it was necessary." Pain is a dangerous emotion that will take you to a place of hatred, manipulation, bitterness, attention seeking, controlling and deceit just to name a few. Be careful not to allow things to fester in your heart and thoughts to occupy your mind. This will cause you to become something or someone people will hate to see coming.

God will allow what you preach and teach to be tried in the fire and tested in the storm, and the human side of who you are will have a reality check for real. Don't think we are exempt from the exam of life. Every experience arrives with a purpose.

Beloved, happiness comes from friends, but joy comes from the LORD. Friends come and go. So does happiness. But joy is everlasting with the LORD.

Chapter 14
Faith through the Fire

A "Piece" of Me

Every mother's heart fills with elation when their bundle of joy comes into the world and the nurse places that sweet baby in her arms. The smell of the beautiful new baby overrides all the labor pains experienced over the previous hours—no matter how many hours the pain lasted. My experience was no exception.

This beautiful, innocent, little life came from the very inner parts of my being, growing daily as it depended on my physical body for nourishment, oxygen supply, and everything. The very essence of life is dependent on the mother carrying this beautiful little life. In the end, it doesn't matter if it's a boy or girl. As a mother we just want a healthy baby with all ten fingers and toes, two eyes, ears, all its limbs, and a beautiful little nose. Hair color isn't important. We don't even care if there's any hair at all. This little life can be bald. From the moment of birth, this life will be loved.

There are no books, parenting guide, or instructions that say "After the Delivery" comes life and the real hard work of taking care of this little child. Nothing says in a few years, that baby won't be little anymore, but a grown adult.

We are never prepared as parents on how to navigate our children through life, but we give them all the wisdom and knowledge we can, understanding that soon they will be adults, making adults decisions. Some far too early before it's time, in our opinion. We try to mentally prepare ourselves to let go and allow our little babies to become grown adults even with life challenges ahead. As hard as we try, we can't protect them from many things in the four letter word called "life." How do we protect our children from all of life's tragedies, mistakes, broken hearts, negative influences, etc.? We pray, we protect, we pray, we protect. And we even give advice with long lectures and drills of how we want them to have better or more and don't want them to experience the hardships we encountered during our growing years or later as parents.

My firstborn, Tori, was a determined young lady, desiring to succeed in life. She was blessed to finish college after the setback with her health. She recovered and did well for several years.

While in college she desired a relationship, but as a mother, nothing or nobody is ever good enough for our daughters. She experienced a relationship she thought was love, and oh did I intervene. I kept telling her, nope, he's not the one. My main concern was for him to be understanding of her health. She was doing very well, and I didn't recommend the stress of dating.

Well after a couple of warning signs, I told her, "He's not the one, but you may have to figure this one out." And I left it alone—after I lectured him a time or two.

The following Christmas (2004), she called me. "Mom, you were right. I'm sorry. I think I'm not ready for a serious relationship. I'm going to focus on my studies and hurry and finish college."

On the other end of the phone, I tried to conceal my excitement, but I didn't really. "Oh, that's wonderful!"

The following year quickly approached, she was home visiting. She came home very frequently, and then suddenly, those visits became short. I didn't mention it. I just kept my antennas up. She bloomed, confident in who she was, a driving force into her future.

Early spring of her junior year of college, we planned a day of shopping. I drove to Huntsville to visit her.

As I pulled up and got out of the car, she stood there, smiling. "Hey Mom, this is my friend."

I raised my eyebrows and looked at the young man. "Oh, ok."

"Really Mom—just a friend."

She introduced me, and her friend left, very nice and a wonderful gentleman.

"Should I be worried?" A mother has to ask such a question.

"No, Mother. I promise we are friends. I'm focused on school, and he's about to graduate within the year."

"Ok. I trust you."

Before long, we went inside, preparing for the shopping trip, and she couldn't wait. "Ok, Mom. Tell me what you think. Do you discern anything strange? What was your first impression?"

I laughed. "I thought he was just a friend. I knew better."

Joy and happiness lit up her face. Her eyes beamed like the sun. I knew—she was in love with her friend. This was something special, and surprisingly, my heart had peace about it.

I waited for her to give me details as the months progressed. She said, "We laugh, talk, and his family is very similar to our family. Everyone is close and loving."

That's all I needed to hear. God bonded us so close together—like a sister, daughter, mother bond. I know that may be hard to explain. We became each other's strength over the years. I leaned on her, and she leaned on me. We talked three or four times a day, as I did with my mother. Tori trusted me, and I trusted her. We're mother/daughter, but something in our relationship shifted, and I was so thankful.

I experienced a health scare in 2005 with abnormal

cancer cells, resulting in surgery with a six-week recovery. Tori was pretty upset with me for not telling her everything.

I explained, "With you in school, I didn't want you to be distracted."

"No, Mother. That's not fair. We promised not to keep secrets."

"Yes. You are absolutely right."

I repented and apologized, and we moved forward. Things were stable at that time. We recently moved into a new home to get the girls into a better school. After a couple of hardships, I was fearful but pursued the change after the girls got older. Previously, I owned two businesses, a dress shop and a restaurant. Both had peak seasons and off-peak seasons. I also worked a full-time job in addition to owning the businesses. I shifted my focus to my full-time job, which had become more demanding with long hours. Yet things remained stable. We moved and settled in Crowley, Texas.

The entire family bubbled with excitement as college graduation quickly approached. As I looked back over all the opposition we faced, there was the day and hour. What the doctor said Tori couldn't do, yet God graced her to complete her college education.

She graduated with a Bachelor's Degree in Criminal Justice in 2007, returned home and accepted a position as a special education teacher while pursuing her Master's Degree in Forensic Psychology. She didn't take to her sixth-grade class too well in the beginning. Her patience with children stretched a little thin, but as time went on, she fell in love with her class.

Some of the students struggled in class, but she took the extra time to help. During the holidays, for those less fortunate, she bought small items such as socks. As winter approached, she purchased hats and gloves.

My heart broke when she told me a story about one young girl who needed some shoes. Tori purchased the shoes over the weekend and gave them to the young girl on the following Monday. Her student was so excited, she gave her a big hug and told her she loved her. After school, the young girl asked if she could leave her shoes locked in the classroom because if she took them home, they might get stolen.

A young boy who was also a student in her class, pulled Tori's hair when he saw her in the hallway.

She said, "Mom, I almost let him have it."

I laughed at the thought. "No, you can't do that. He admires you."

She developed a joy of teaching and loved the classroom—especially with special needs children. She told me it was very rewarding. She bloomed in her teaching while working on her second degree. This child of mine was so ambitious, her drive was over the top. I guess that's why I had a very hard time listening to people complain about why they couldn't work with a backache, toothache, or headache. Although in remission, Tori still had her challenges and days of being tired, but she never let that stop her. I encouraged her not to overdo or stress out. She had goals and plans to pursue, and she loved having her own paycheck and money. She worked on Saturdays at different youth sporting events, driving far and near to make extra money. She was a very hard worker.

Soon I started hearing hints about rings, dresses and houses. Ok, prepare me now.

As I shared earlier, her friend, then her best friend, became her fiancé. They fell in love and were inseparable. Soon we had an engagement and made wedding plans. She and the love of her life married in December 2008.

During this time, things were a little tight for me financially. However, I had it in my heart to host the dream wedding she desired. She had a vision and desire for the wedding, and she was so determined. We spent weekends shopping for dresses, looking at venues, talking to caterers, and picking out wedding cakes. What a joy we experienced.

I prayed, "Lord, give me the financial means to give my daughter the wedding she desires."

As the wedding date drew near, the vision was coming into fruition. She wanted everything presented in top perfection. I guess I didn't realize the full extent of her dream fairytale wedding. Wow. She ordered goldfish and this clear tall vase for her centerpieces.

White feathers accented the décor on the tables for the reception. All the pieces came together. We attended Bridal Expos, and we had time to take a breather and enjoy a beautiful bridal shower.

The wedding day arrived, every detail beyond my expectation. Some dear friends stepped in to help coordinate and decorate. The evening was beautiful. We engraved so much of ourselves into all the planning. Then soon the lovely couple left on their honeymoon.

Now, remember, she was still in school, planning a wedding and teaching school. I was concerned she was taking on too much stress.

Soon after the wedding and honeymoon, everything settled down from all the excitement of the festivities. We finally relaxed. She had MaKayla taking an interest in basketball. In addition, she helped with school projects, assisted me with picking her sisters up from aftercare. She was such a great help to me, advising me on academics, school, activities and programs for her little sisters.

One day, while sitting at my desk at work, I received a text message. I couldn't make it all the way out, but I said, "This looks like a pregnancy test. No this can't be."

I called her so fast. "Girl, what is this?"

She laughed. I didn't see the humor in it.

I immediately told her to make an appointment with the doctor and we did. Soon after we were advised she needed to see a high-risk OB/GYN. We were able to get in within the following week.

We were excited, but I was extremely concerned. Still, I sure didn't let her know.

The doctor shared his thoughts and concerns but didn't see any reason why she couldn't try to carry the baby. On the other hand, her Rheumatologist was more concerned and wanted to make sure she understood the risks of the Lupus flaring back up. He didn't want to aggravate any symptoms because she had been doing so well.

All was well, up until one Friday evening. She didn't feel well but assured me she was just tired.

I suggested, "Let's just go get checked out at the ER and make sure everything is ok."

She agreed. Once there, they called her doctor, and he asked them to keep her overnight for observation. Because the OB/GYN didn't work through Baylor All Saints, she had to be transferred to Harris Methodist downtown. An on-call doctor came to visit and began running tests. He suggested treating the Lupus he thought might have flared up. He wasn't sure, and the specialist wasn't there to tell us anything.

On Monday, we discovered they had given her a substantial amount of steroids, which extended her stay due to the medication. The steroids compromised her immune system. Nevertheless, she was excited every moment she was able to hear the baby's heartbeat.

What was supposed to be one day turned into three weeks. Every day it was something different. Not in pain, she worked on lesson plans, preparing tests for her students, talking to the principal, working on homework for her classes and studying. So there was no major sign to indicate something going wrong.

Upon observing her for three weeks, the pregnancy and Lupus raged a war in her body, the Lupus as a strong enemy of her body and the baby's as well. It caused stress on her kidneys. The doctors advised her and her husband the time might come when they had to make some drastic decisions regarding the baby and her. She couldn't think of anything else but the baby. That little life meant everything to her.

When her Lupus diagnosis was made while she was in high school, we visited different specialists. Some told us she would never conceive. With concerns of chemotherapy as part of the treatment, we were advised of all the risk factors.

Just the thought that she conceived this little miracle was an amazing gift, and her heart was completely taken by this infant growing inside of her. As mothers, we want to guide, instruct and direct. For me, this point and time were a little different than before because she was married. It was important for me to allow her husband to be her strength. Although I never left her side, staying there the entire time, I respected his place and position. I gave support and advice when asked. I listened as the doctors gave their medical advice and opinion, which was hard to hear as we took in words disheartening to our faith and what we trusted God to do.

Beyond Devastation – I AM BEYOND Devastated

After much prayer and believing for a miracle, God chose something different. Early Friday morning March 12, 2009, the little precious life my daughter longed to carry and give birth to lost the battle, and they whisked my daughter to surgery. After hours of waiting, the doctor walked into the waiting room, prepared to give us news we didn't want to accept.

"I'm sorry, about the baby," he said with a soothing tone. "Your daughter will be in recovery. We will let you know when you can see her."

I went back to her room and fell in the floor releasing the loudest scream of my life. At this same time, my second marriage was in turmoil. It had been for over a year. I felt numb, alone, angry.

I made up in my mind, "I'm not going home with the same pain and issue. I just lost my grandbaby, and I'm mad as hell."

Yes, that's exactly what I said. No words could articulate my emotions. I tried to get all my crying out before I saw my daughter. What I planned to say, how I was going to look her in the eyes. I felt like I failed her—somehow this was all my fault. I know God allows things to happen, but processing this one required more than I had.

After returning to her room, Tori was still under sedation. Filled with sadness, she asked what the doctor said. I shared the news—so devastating to hear the words come out of my mouth and ring in my ears.

I stood by her bedside. "The most important thing right now is to get you well. You will bounce back, and there will be another opportunity to have a baby."

I've never seen such sadness in her eyes. Mothers are supposed to be able to take the pain away, protect their children, and comfort them when they hurt. I felt so helpless, like there was nothing I could do to make her feel better. This shattered my heart even more.

I did the only thing I knew to do—I uttered a silent prayer. "Lord, where are you? Help us please!"

Later that evening, Tori's Rheumatologist stopped by. He and the OB/GYN specialist discussed her care and loss of the baby. After he visited with her, he told me to step outside in the hall.

Seriousness covered his face. "Your daughter is not out of the woods yet."

Emotionally she was in a tough place, but I thought physically she was okay. "I'm not sure what you are talking about."

"She has an infection in her lungs."

"Well, for the last two days, she kept asking me to look at her throat. She told me her throat was hurting, and she complained to the nurse several times."

Although still in the middle of flu season, we never gave it a second thought since she was in the hospital.

The doctor listened intently. "We'll be watching her closely."

Later that evening, she wanted to walk around. We laughed a little and cracked jokes. I told her I would let her rest and be back in the morning. Her husband and I took shifts staying overnight with her.

I went up the next day, and she wasn't feeling her best. She didn't like the medication they gave her, saying it made her too sleepy. I asked them not to give it to her again. From that point on, she just wasn't herself. I knew she hurt from the loss of the baby.

Early Sunday morning, we were informed she had pneumonia. They gave her medication to help with the infection, but by Monday, she took a turn for the worse. I spent as much time at the hospital as I could between working. During my lunch break, I went to check on her and promised I would be back soon.

Near the end of my work day, she texted me. *Mom, can you come?*

I quickly texted back. *Yes I'm on the way*

In my mind, she was going to bounce back and get better in a day or two. I never imagined she would get so sick at a rapid pace.

The Night Shift

Once I was off work that evening, I went back to the hospital. I didn't like the way she sounded. "Tori, let me go home, get your sisters ready for bed, get some clothes, and I will be back in an hour."

I did just that, not wasting a moment or lingering for long. I stayed with her that night, sitting in the chair next to her bed as she coughed and coughed and coughed.

I finally walked out to the nurse's station, asking if there was anything they could do. "She's been coughing for two days. She's getting weaker by the minute, and she's not resting due to the cough."

They called the doctor (OB/GYN) several times. As time went on through the night, they gave her a couple of breathing treatments, which didn't help at all. As I look back on things, the clock seemed to move slowly. I remember each hour and what happened within the hour. My heart crushing, the sound of her cough scarred my soul, pierced my heart like a knife.

Around 3 a.m., I said, "Ok, enough!"

I got mad, walked out to the nurses' station again, and demanded she call the doctor. He gave some instructions and requested a couple of tests. Without hesitation, they took her to ICU. By the time we got to the floor, she was in distress. I walked and paced the floor as they tried to get her settled. Her condition declined rapidly. I stayed by her side along with her husband to keep her calm. She knew something was wrong as she asked questions about her levels, her oxygen, and her blood gas. She knew it was bad. She struggled, every breath getting harder and harder.

I called my sister and told her what was going on.

"I'm on the way," she replied.

I constantly kept saying, "Tori, just hold on. It's going to be ok. Hold on, baby. It's going to be ok."

The nurse came in the room and explained she was going to try a different mask to help get air into Tori's lungs. That actually made things worse. Because of the fluid in her lungs, Tori was literally suffocating. I still remember the beeping sounds of the machines, the glass door of the ICU Room, and I held by my baby for dear life.

Finally, I let out this scream, "HELP MY BABY!"

It felt like everyone took their time. The nurses changed shifts. It was the worst experience.

Before the break of day, I grabbed the phone to call her dad, but there was no answer. Surely he has to get here. Our baby is slipping away. I kept dialing the number but nothing. Am I dialing the right number?

As my voice lifted in rage and echoed throughout the halls of ICU, my sister took over and called Tori's dad.

She spoke into the phone. "We need you, and that's it."

Minutes later he was there by her side, watching the

doctors fight for our baby girl.

Tori grabbed the mask and snatched it off. "Momma, I can't breathe."

I held on to her tightly. "I got you."

I glanced over at her husband, tears cascading down his face as I tried to be strong for both of them. The last thing I remember is her eyes closing and her arm growing lifeless as I held her.

Suddenly, the nurses all ran in, commanding us to leave the room. I knew in my gut we were losing her.

I went down the hall and screamed, "LORD, NO!" I stretched in the floor and literally felt a virtue of life leave my body as if I could feel Tori leaving me.

My sister walked in and heard me screaming down the hall. She just laid in the floor with me, not saying anything, but comforting me with her presence.

I don't recall how long they worked to revive my daughter. It was a horror to watch.

I heard words no mother wants to hear, yet trying to process those words felt like a nightmare I couldn't wake from. "We will work on her as long as you tell us. We won't stop, but it looks grave. We believe she suffered a form of a stroke or blood clot due to pneumonia."

My baby and grandbaby both gone, my life SHATTERED in a million pieces.

What kind of hand has life dealt me? What did I do so awful to deserve this horror of pain? I can't tell you how much time passed. Eventually, my son-in-law and I made the decision to battle no more. The Lupus and all the complications that came with it defeated our faith, even as we believed God for a miracle.

Hearing the doctors announce the time of death of my sweet 24-year-old daughter was the most horrific experience of my life. To feel the lifeline cut off from the beautiful soul I gave birth to goes beyond words, the ache of my heart incomprehensible.

By early morning, the hospital filled with friends and family from far and near. Now the challenge lay before me to tell my father—the little girl he helped me raise was gone.

My dad's world centered around his grandchildren. My sister called some family members, asking them to go to his house, pick him up and bring him to the hospital. The nightmare raged on. Literally broken mentally, shattered in fact, my thoughts no longer lived in my mind. My brain function was no longer capable of processing in a normal manner.

Marriage in shambles, my daughter gone, and a grandbaby I never got to meet no longer existed, causing normal brain functions to shut down. Once home I had to deliver the news to MaKayla and Jaslin.

How do I tell these two little girls, who look up to their sister and were so excited about the baby?

MaKayla actually wrote a report for English about the wonderful life event of becoming an auntie when her sister delivers the new baby. She got an A on her report. How could I explain something I barely comprehended myself?

This took a toll on both the girls, but especially MaKayla. She always wanted Tori to be proud of whatever she did. Tori loved basketball and introduced MaKayla to the game, although MaKayla knew nothing about it. Months later it became very therapeutic during her grief process.

Tomorrow Will Come

My feet never fail. When oceans rise my soul rests in Your embrace, Lord. We all know death is part of life, but we must live until we die. Song of Solomon 8:6 says, *"Place me like a seal over your heart, like a seal on your arm; for love is as strong as death, its jealousy unyielding as the grave. It burns like blazing fire, like a mighty flame."* (NIV)

The death and loss of a child are frequently called the ultimate tragedy. Nothing can be more devastating. Along with the usual symptoms and stages of grief, many other issues make parental bereavement particularly difficult to resolve. And this grief over the loss of a child can be exacerbated and complicated by feelings of injustice—the understandable feeling this loss never should have happened.

During the early days of grieving, I experienced excruciating pain, alternating with numbness—a dichotomy that may persist for months or longer. Many parents who lost their son or daughter report they feel they can only "exist" and every motion or need beyond that seems nearly impossible. For me, as with many other parents, coping with the death and loss of a child requires some of the hardest work one will ever have to do.

Surviving the death and loss of a child takes dedication to life. As a parent, you gave birth to live as a promise to the future. After that child's death, you must make a new commitment to living, as hard or impossible as it may seem in the tragic aftermath.

You will survive this loss. However, the experience will change you forever.

Expect Restoration After a Loss

A broken heart can be healed. Unfulfilled dreams can become the greatest source of hope. You can learn so much about hope from the Book of Ruth. She was not afraid to step out of her comfort zone and embrace new possibilities. She ventured past cultural limitations to discover a life of fulfillment, willing to risk it all and stretch her faith.

I went an entire year before my spiritual mother said to me, "I have walked and carried you as far as I know how with the help of the Lord. Now we need some reinforcement. It's time for someone who can help you on a professional level." She paused and let that sink in for a moment. "I have carried you in prayer.

We've talked and prayed. The time has come where you need to speak with a grief counselor."

Of course, she had one in mind and had already reached out to her. I was uncomfortable in the beginning. It took me some time to process and accept I needed the help, but by that time I really needed the help.

I was bitter, angry, feeling guilty. I wasn't eating or sleeping. Nothing made sense to me. I kept replaying that day in my head, mentally tormenting myself by battling with the past. My mind wandered back to the day I took the pills, not wanting to be a teen mother, and the shame I experienced. All these emotions fought against me left and right, leaving no peace nor a moment of solitude.

I took a leave of absence from work, was on medication, couldn't drive and couldn't remember where I put stuff. A part of my brain stopped functioning. I hated going toward the side of town where the hospital was located and avoided it if at all possible.

That made up part of my grief. How you grieve over the death and loss of a child and for how long will be different than for anyone else—you need to allow yourself to grieve in your own way. It must be remembered that bereaved parents can mourn the death of a child of any age. It feels unnatural to outlive a child. It does not make a difference whether your child is four or twenty-four, the age of my daughter when she passed away. The emotion is the same.

All bereaved parents lose a part of themselves, part of their identity. I had to remember I was still a mother. I had two other children who called me Mom, but I felt like I was no longer a mother because I failed one of my children. I couldn't help her. I didn't fight hard enough. I should have spoken up sooner. Every emotion you can imagine ran through my mind.

It Starts Today

I didn't know what to expect on the day of my first session of grief counseling. It made me a little more comfortable that I knew of her and who she was. The first step was hard, walking through the door, agreeing to accept the help.

After the first thirty minutes, Mrs. Cunningham said, "Ok, ma'am. We must identify the type of grief."

Immediately she identified my situation as complicated grief. I experienced the loss of my mother, and I'm a mother who lost a child and grandchild and then also separated in the midst of a divorce. So let's dissect this—grieving the loss of a child, grandchild, marriage, my mother, and later the relationship with my son-in-law. He eventually moved out and on with his life.

The darkest second hour was cleaning out her apartment, packing up her clothes, the first Christmas, which I didn't want to celebrate.

But a dear friend said, "We are coming to decorate your house." And they brought beautifully wrapped gifts for my younger two children.

Sad to say, my pain caused me to neglect them in many areas. I'm thankful for the friends who encouraged me as they helped keep a sense of balance in the girls' lives. I'm so thankful for the memories Tori and I created and shared together. Those memories are what got me through many hard days.

I faced several years of ups and downs, learning to trust God again and walk in God's power and strength. It wasn't easy.

I searched for meaning in my child's death, an understanding of how death fits into the scheme of life. This is too difficult and the answers unattainable. My faith was and still is a source of comfort. Yet at the same time, I battled the feeling of being betrayed by God. I was confused and questioned many things I believed to be certain in my relationship with Him.

I spoke with a father dealing with the death of a child. He shared with me that his faith in life, in general, had been shattered. He long believed that if you lived your life as a good person, striving to make a positive contribution to the world, life would turn out well. The death of his son robbed him of that belief.

This reaction isn't uncommon. Losing a child feels like the ultimate violation of the rules of life.

I told God, "You could have taken a drug addict off the street in place of my child, a murderer, or child molester. Why did it have to be this innocent life? Why did she suffer and have her precious life cut short?" That day tears streamed down my cheeks. Full of anger, I continued. "I will never step in the church again, and I'm not encouraging or ministering Your Word. You allowed this pain to hurt me beyond my wildest dreams."

A quiet voice answered me back. "Her assignment on earth was to die that someone else might live. She had an assignment on earth and made more difference in her 24 years than anyone could in an entire lifetime."

The empty room, the empty chair, the empty car—the empty, the empty, the empty. She left me, and my life was empty.

I sobbed. "How can I face tomorrow with the heartbreak of today? I'm willing, but I'm weak."

I realized I couldn't get this grief process done by myself. I was determined then to work harder during my counseling sessions. I worked at being honest. As each discussion and session peeled me like an onion, layer after layer had to be addressed. Six months into counseling, I worked, I cried, I got angry, and I was depressed. But I was getting the help and doing the work, so I could be a better mother for the children that remained and a better daughter and sister.

I was shattered, but the pieces of my life shifted.

Some pieces didn't fit anymore, and I had to accept it and be ok with that. Some pieces came back together, and some didn't. The pieces that had to be swept away were very important pieces. I tried to force pieces back into place, but they no longer belonged in my life. Forcing a marriage that ended in divorce, forcing financial issues to work that weren't my fault, but it happened. From the test to the testimony, God kept me and my sanity.

My finances plummeted, my home on the verge of foreclosure, and the life insurance company refused to pay the benefits of my daughter's death. All of these circumstances complicated the grief process.

Things turned around a couple of years later. I was able to keep my home, get a new car, and life, in general, looked up.

The Sun Shines through the Son

One of my favorite songs is, "He Thought I was Worth Saving." Music became a passion, getting me through many nights, therapeutic for me. God put a new song in my heart, and He restored my soul.

We may never understand why God allows our paths in life to face so much disappointment and pain. My trust in Him assures me He foreknew all we would go through, and He knows how much we can bear.

I encourage you today, do the work of processing through your grief, no matter if it was yesterday, last week or years ago when you lost your loved one. The work is vital and important to triumph over the pain and to live a life from Broken 2 Blessed. I'm blessed with two beautiful daughters, a husband that loves me, and I'm part of a ministry that is not just a people who assemble together weekly—they are my true family.

During the days I threw in the towel and wanted no longer to live, one person surprised me with their actions of love and support and words that moved me forward.

"You can't stop. Your faith is stronger than anyone I know. You must continue to be a light in the world and live for your daughter. Dance in the rain as if there is no tomorrow." My childhood sweetheart, Tori's father came through when I needed him most.

He is now my husband. After twenty years, five with no communication, the loss of our daughter brought us back together. As we stood over her casket during our one-on-one time with her, that last moment of privacy before the funeral gave us the opportunity to laugh, hug, forgive.

We spent many hours together at the hospital, sometimes in total silence, but to share time with our daughter who needed us. We sat all the differences of our past aside to be the fortified strength for her. In her last days, she saw us hold hands, comfort and support each other. And I believe that made her heart smile. Days after, we tried to remember why we stopped talking. How did we get to that point? The death of our daughter brought our lives together again.

Many asked, "Were you guys grieving and found that you needed each other?"

Well yes, that goes without saying. We were able to be the outlet and strength. Only we could understand each other's pain of the heart as parents.

As I conclude this writing I must share, I discovered many things from my shattered place. After my healing process, I began to write this book and went back to school. I'm in tune with my purpose through my pain — to push the next person into their purpose in life. You might call me a "PURPOSE PUSHER."

I discovered the love to travel, try new foods, and discover new ideas. Mother's Day is usually the hardest holiday for me, still very difficult at times. My healing to love Mother's Day again came when I researched and found a place to take my daughter's wedding dress. They have little christening gowns made for premature infants. These little, white silk gowns are donated to the NICU of various hospitals, the most rewarding and fulfilling moment of my healing process.

I also donated her nice clothes, many with price tags still on them, to a battered women's shelter and a store that allowed women to shop for free who need clothes for a job interview. Once I made the decision to let go and not hold on to the baggage of my pain, many new doors and new things happened in my life. God allowed so many young people to come into my life, many of them call me Mom or Momma. God gave me double love for my loss.

Piece by Peace

I'm happy from the inside out. First from the peace of God, remembering I'm only human like the next person. When life touches you, and at some time it WILL touch you, it must be dealt with. I no longer make excuses. I made a choice to process and work through the grief of my life, and you can too.

Hot coffee as the substance of my favorite mug splattered all over the floor. In the midst of the hurried cleaning frenzy, I lost my grip. It crashed to the floor, breaking into an explosion of pieces—beyond repair. My favorite coffee mug, gone—swept into the trash.

"Should have been more careful," I muttered, beating myself up.

So it is in real life.

"Just glue it back Mom," my girls said.

But it would never be the same. The damage was done.

Broken things. Very familiar to a family of five with a dog, rabbit and hamster. Lots of things moving around and active in our house. And if certain broken pieces are able to be fixed, they normally find a temporary home on the shelf, awaiting the super glue repairs. Or maybe just tossed away in the drawer if unable to be neatly pieced back together and strategically repaired without a hint of patchwork, cracks of super glue lines. Often, it takes too much work to fix what is broken. It's easier to just buy a new one.

Ever feel that way? Broken. Shattered. Set on a shelf. Tossed aside. Or thrown away. Forgotten about, feeling you have no worth or value. Restoration—even an attempt—takes too much work.

"Just get a new one," the mindset of our culture. "Don't let anyone see the broken flaws." Such reality in the way we often live in this world. What happens when what you once had can't be replaced? It lost its value. This is where you come to the reality of who you are—a person of substance. Like the mug, which contained steaming hot coffee, was designed to weather extreme temperature, so are you.

While watching an antique art show, I learned in Japan they've made an art out of restoring broken things. An ancient practice called Kintsugi, meaning "golden joinery" or "to patch with gold," is an age-old custom of repairing cracked pottery with real gold, not only fixing the break, but greatly increasing the value of the piece. What an amazing discovery.

At the heart of it all—turning what is broken into beautiful, cherished pieces by sealing the cracks and crevices with lines of fine gold. Instead of hiding flaws, they create a whole new design and bring unique beauty to the original piece. The pottery actually becomes more beautiful and valuable in the restoration process because, though it was once broken, it not only has history, but also a new story. I was overwhelmed with gratitude while learning something new. This was a lightbulb moment for me.

While most normal repairs of broken things hide themselves, like nicely sealed super glue fixes, the usual intent is simply to make something "as good as new." Yet the art of Kintsugi reinforces a profound belief that the repair can make things not only as good as before but "better than new."

Better than new. Come on soak that in. Meditate on that for a minute. Yes, exciting! It's all coming together. The break made me better. My value just went up.

The lies and tricks our mind tend to make us think in our deep and most vulnerable weak moments, when we've lost our grip on life, and things come crashing down. We feel the need to hide the scars. We feel like the brokenness rendered us useless in life. You may feel beyond repair this time. You feel tossed aside. Forgotten. Shamed. Rejected—as you sit on a shelf collecting dust.

Yet God breaks through all that mess. You are never beyond healing. You are never too broken for restoration. You are never too shattered for repair. Don't be ashamed of your scars, of the deep crevices that line your soul, or the broken places of your life. They have an amazing story to tell.

Here is truth. Just because we've been broken doesn't mean we are thrown away. Just because we've been broken doesn't mean we are un-usable, set up on a shelf. Just because we've been broken doesn't mean we are forgotten.

Throw your hands up and scream, "I'm Better Than New! The break made me better."

Take control of your shattered pieces, and gain the PEACE of your life back.

Today you are EMPOWERED not just as a survivor of the shattered pieces—you are empowered to overcome and conquer, to turn obstacles into opportunities to be the man or woman you were destined to be.

What you make happen for someone else, God will make happen for you. So make it happen.

Be careful of the words that are released out of your mouth for they are spirit and life. Once they are released into the atmosphere, they bring forth life or death.

About the Author

Mrs. Helena Lewis-Norman is the proud daughter of Henry Lewis and the late Joyce Lewis of Fort Worth, TX. She is the wife of Mr. Gerald Norman and the mother of MaKayla and Jaslin Johnson and the late Sha'Toriya Lewis-Foley. Along with her sister LaJoyce Timmons and two older brothers, Anthony and John Lewis, Helena was raised in a household deeply rooted in love and faith. Their parents taught them always to do unto others as you will have them do unto you.

Helena was reared in Fort Worth, Texas in the Riverside Community, where everyone is considered family. Upon graduation from Amon-Carter Riverside High School, she attended Tarrant County College, pursuing a degree in Business Management and completed Medical Coding School. Helena worked for Alcon Laboratories for 27 years.

As a teenager, she received salvation and loved serving in her local church, Friendly Temple Church of God in Christ, where she grew up under the leadership of Superintendent R. C. Williams for over 30 years. In 1995 Helena accepted her call into ministry that was revealed and evident upon her life. In 1998 she began ministering the Word of God. By 2002, she accepted her call as an Evangelist. The mantle of prayer and compassion for others was part of the legacy and teaching instilled by her biological mother. Understanding that serving with the heart of a servant is most important, she strives to help others live a life of wholeness from inside out. With emotional healing and spiritual restoration, God began to use her in a special way through the wisdom of the Word of God and life experiences of personal pain and unexpected life circumstances. Her pain became her passion for the pursuit of helping and encouraging parents who grieve the loss of a child.

Being ordained as a Licensed Minister and after proper training and mentorship by her Spiritual Mother, the late Prophetess Trinia James, Helena began walking in her call with a new measure of boldness and authority. With much prayer and fasting in 2011, Helena accepted the position of interim Pastor of Spring Time International Ministries. She then put her personal ministry and goals on hold temporarily to assist with carrying the ministry and vision of Spring Time, which is now Refiner's Fire "RHEMA" Ministries, where she serves as Senior Pastor. Again, God began to awaken the Evangelist for a greater work. In 2015, "HSN Ministries" was birthed. Since that time, God has used her to travel, preaching, teaching and prophesying the unadulterated Word of God across denominational boundaries with an unquestionable anointing. She is a spiritual advisor to many and a rising prophetic voice to the nations.

Pastor Helena Norman has been afforded the opportunity to serve on the board of Kingdom Covenant Ministries under the leadership of Bishop Donald Butler. Currently, Pastor Helena is serving under the covering of Bishop Kevin and Pastor Sonjia Dickerson. A new chapter of Pastor Helena's life unfolded when she married the love of her life Mr. Gerald Norman in January 2013.

"The Spirit of the Lord is upon me, because he hath anointed me to preach the gospel to the poor; he hath sent me to heal the brokenhearted, to preach deliverance to the captives, and recovering of sight to the blind, to set at liberty them that are bruised, to preach the acceptable year of the Lord (Luke 4:18-19 KJV)."

God blessed Pastor Helena Norman with many spiritual sons and daughters. It is with great delight she develops and cultivates the next generation for such a time as this. Her greatest joy is being a mother to her wonderful daughters, grooming them for their God-given Purpose.